MAKING *elegant* Custom Tables

DOUG STOWE

POPULAR WOODWORKING BOOKS

CINCINNATI, OHIO

www.popularwoodworking.com

READ THIS IMPORTANT SAFETY NOTICE

To prevent accidents, keep safety in mind while you work. Use the safety guards installed on power equipment; they are for your protection. When working on power equipment, keep fingers away from saw blades, wear safety goggles to prevent injuries from flying wood chips and sawdust, wear headphones to protect your hearing, and consider installing a dust vacuum to reduce the amount of airborne sawdust in your woodshop. Don't wear loose clothing, such as neckties or shirts with loose sleeves, or jewelry, such as rings, necklaces or bracelets, when working on power equipment. Tie back long hair to prevent it from getting caught in your equipment. People who are sensitive to certain chemicals should check the chemical content of any product before using it. The authors and editors who compiled this book have tried to make the contents as accurate and correct as possible. Plans, illustrations, photographs and text have been carefully checked. All instructions, plans and projects should be carefully read, studied and understood before beginning construction. Due to the variability of local conditions, construction materials, skill levels, etc., neither the author nor Popular Woodworking Books assumes any responsibility for any accidents, injuries, damages or other losses incurred resulting from the material presented in this book.

METRIC CONVERSION CHART

TO CONVERT	TO	MULTIPLY BY
Inches	Centimeters	2.54
Centimeters	Inches	0.4
Feet	Centimeters	30.5
Centimeters	Feet	0.03
Yards	Meters	0.9
Meters	Yards	1.1
Sq. Inches	Sq. Centimeters	6.45
Sq. Centimeters	Sq. Inches	0.16
Sq. Feet	Sq. Meters	0.09
Sq. Meters	Sq. Feet	10.8
Sq. Yards	Sq. Meters	0.8
Sq. Meters	Sq. Yards	1.2
Pounds	Kilograms	0.45
Kilograms	Pounds	2.2
Ounces	Grams	28.4
Grams	Ounces	0.04

Visit our Web site at www.popularwoodworking.com for information and more resources for woodworkers.

Other fine Popular Woodworking Books are available from your local bookstore or direct from the publisher.

06 05 04 03 02   5 4 3 2 1

Library of Congress Cataloging-in-Publication Data

Stowe, Doug.
　Making elegant custom tables / by Doug Stowe
　　　p. cm.
　Includes index.
　ISBN 1-55870-565-1 (alk. paper)
　　1. Tables--Design and construction. 2. Woodwork. I. Title.

　TT197.5.T3 S77 2001
　684.1'3--dc21　　　　　　　　　2001035281

Acquisitions Editor: Jim Stack
Edited by Jennifer Churchill
Content edited by Michael Berger
Designed by Brian Roeth
Interior layout by Kathy Bergstrom
Production coordinated by Emily Gross
Illustrations by Graham Blackburn
Step-by-step photography by Doug Stowe
Cover and chapter lead photography by Allen Smith
Editorial assistance by Megan Williamson

ABOUT THE AUTHOR

Doug Stowe is a self-employed furniture craftsman, writer and teacher specializing in the creative and responsible use of American hardwoods.

He lives on a wooded hillside at the edge of Eureka Springs, Arkansas, where he draws strength and inspiration for his work from lasting friendship.

To learn more about the author and his work, please visit his Web site at www.dougstowe.com.

ACKNOWLEDGEMENTS

My thanks to the following who have given me the opportunity to make tables:

C.J. Appel
Susan Beard and Mel Robinson
Beverly Cruthirds and Richard Owen
Mike and Laura Dumontier
Jean Elderwind and Lucy Stowe
Robert Ely and Linda Jennings
Paul Harvel and the Little Rock
    Area Chamber of Commerce
Mary Lou (Wuzzie) and Newton
    Heston Jr.
Jack and Martha Leary
Eleanor Lux and Bob Wilson
Rick and Kathy McCormick
Chuck and Ramona McNeal
Jim and Susan Nelson
Dorothy Stowe
Kent and Karen Swogger
Mary Lou Taylor and Michael Goldstein
C.D. Wright
Josephine and Leslie Gyuro

Thanks to the following friends in Eureka Springs who provided settings and props for photography:
Lucilla Garrett for the use of No. 2
    Cottage
Jim Wallace and Laura Waters —
    Paradise Pottery
The Palace Hotel and Bath House
Mary Ellen Sheard — Crystal Gardens
    Antiques

Special thanks to my editor, Mike Berger; my photographer, Allen Smith; illustrator Graham Blackburn; the staff at Popular Woodworking Books; Kreg Tool Company; and Lee Valley/Veritas Tools.

This book is dedicated to the people in my small town of Eureka Springs, Arkansas, for their encouragement of fine work, their dedication to preservation and the quality of their friendship.

table of contents

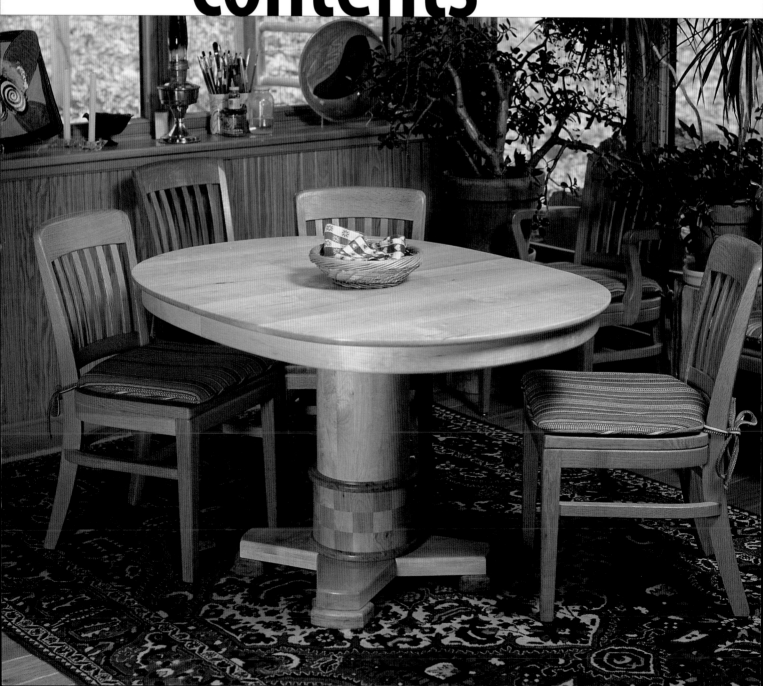

introduction

Chairs and beds hold the human body in positions of comfort. Cabinets store and organize our collections of things, lest they clutter and overwhelm us. Tables, on the other hand, display the important things in our lives in places where they can be seen, used more fully and appreciated more deeply. In a sense, tables create for humankind the opportunity to regard things as sacred in the material world, lifting them above and holding them separate from the bare earth.

It is not surprising that tables fulfill such an important spiritual function in our daily lives. They are the places upon which meals are served. They are the modern hearths around which families gather. Things are displayed upon them that inform those friends and relatives who enter our homes who we are as human beings. In addition, tables have become art, expressing whimsy, grace, humor and beauty, as they stretch our imaginations to embrace new concepts in design and the relationship of material and form.

I've been making tables for as long as I've worked with wood. Each was designed for a friend with special needs and desires. Some have been decorative, some simple. Each has been made to be used and enjoyed.

In writing this book, it is my hope as I make these custom tables that I may share with you the process through which they are created. A custom table is by its very nature unique. You may follow the steps offered here to make these tables for your own home. It is my hope that the examples these tables offer will give you the confidence to create tables of your own design and to meet the needs and desires of people you love.

I have chosen the projects in this book to illustrate a variety of techniques for table construction. These techniques can be used to create whatever comes from your own imagination and relationships with family and friends.

The possibilities are without end. Tables can be simple or ornate, functional or purely decorative. They can also be easy and fun to make.

victorian **tea table**

I live in a small community in northwest Arkansas that was founded in 1880 as people gathered around springs that were thought to offer healing of mind, body and spirit. Now the entire city of Eureka Springs is on the National Register of Historic Places, and the homes and buildings of the Victorian age are protected and preserved for the pride of residents and the enjoyment of guests. The famous springs have become polluted and their waters are no longer safe for drinking, but the small-town atmosphere and community spirit in a place where the past is treasured and people take time for one another have allowed Eureka Springs to continue to be a place of healing.

This table is a little tribute to my small Victorian community and also a way to illustrate a few simple techniques for table-making. The tapered sliding dovetails used to assemble the various parts to the central column give a great deal of strength and stability to the table. This tea table, like many of my projects, originated as a simple pencil sketch on a notepad. The final design and shape were allowed to emerge as the table traveled through its various stages.

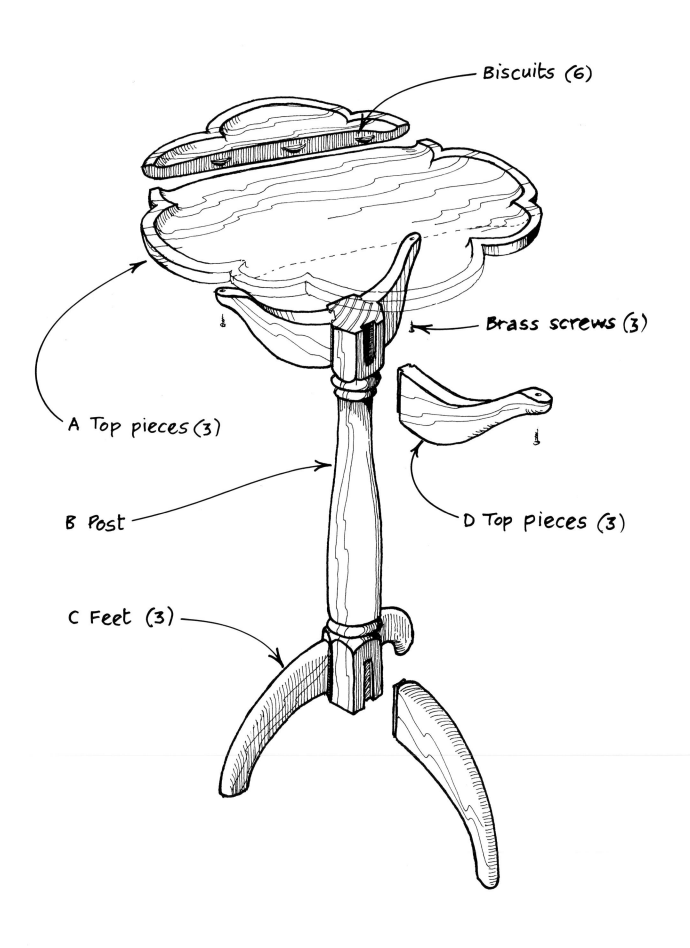

Biscuits (6)

Brass screws (3)

A Top pieces (3)

D Top Pieces (3)

B Post

C Feet (3)

CUTTING LIST (INCHES) • victorian tea table

REF.	QTY.	PART	STOCK	THICKNESS	WIDTH	LENGTH	COMMENTS
A	3	Top pieces	Walnut	$7/8$	$6^{1}/4$	$18^{1}/2$	
B	I	Post	Walnut	$2^{7}/8$	$2^{7}/8$	19	
D	3	Top support pieces	Walnut	I	$2^{1}/4$	8	Shape from stock $2^{1}/4$" x 9"; angles on ends are 65° and 25°
C	3	Feet	Walnut	I	3	10	Shape from stock $3^{1}/4$" x 12" w/45° angle at each end.

Hardware and Supplies

	3	No. 6 x $1^{1}/2$" brass screws
	6	No. 20 biscuits
		Spray adhesive
		Danish oil

CUTTING LIST (MILLIMETERS) • victorian tea table

REF.	QTY.	PART	STOCK	THICKNESS	WIDTH	LENGTH	COMMENTS
A	3	Top pieces	Walnut	22	158	470	
B	I	Post	Walnut	75	75	485	
D	3	Top support pieces	Walnut	25	60	200	Shape from stock 60mm x 23mm; angles on ends are 65° and 25°
C	3	Feet	Walnut	25	75	250	Shape from stock 75mm x 305mm w/45° angle at each end.

Hardware and Supplies

	3	No. 6 x 38mm brass screws
	6	No. 20 biscuits
		Spray adhesive
		Danish oil

CUTTING TO "FIT"

There is a temptation for beginning woodworkers to take cutting lists and, in the enthusiasm of starting a new project, attempt to cut all the pieces at once to the dimensions offered by the author. As a word of caution, and in the interest of your success, the best advice of an experienced woodworker is: Even when cutting lists are perfect, they don't take into consideration all the concerns of "fit," which are beyond the realm of careful measurement. For instance, if I were to cut a piece to length, then cut a 1" tenon on each end, I have three opportunities for the measurement to be slightly off from what was intended in a plan. These small variations can add up and become significant in the look of a finished piece. Whether making a box, a table, a home or a castle, it is best to cut the parts in a gradual manner, as required to "fit" as the work evolves. Small mistakes, such as a piece cut $1/64$" too long, or $1/32$" too short can be adjusted in the subsequent parts giving a "perfect" result to an imperfect process.

1 Alternate the orientation of the annual rings to prevent the tabletop from warping. Here I've marked the rings in chalk for better visibility, and I've marked the arrangement of boards for reassembly and gluing. I use Xs to mark the bark side of the stock and Os to mark the center or heart side. The triangle lines are used to establish the order of reassembly.

2 Use a biscuit joiner and No. 20 biscuits. Although No. 20 biscuits aren't necessary for strength, they help greatly in the alignment of the boards.

3 To make the top from narrower stock, use biscuits, glue and clamps. Let the glue set up before removing the clamps.

4 Use your paper-cutting skills to create the shape for the finished tabletop. Use an old paper grocery sack, cut out a square shape to match the glued-up top, then fold it in half, quarters and then eighths from the center point. (Shown here is my second attempt; my first was too ornate.) Glue the paper to the tabletop stock using spray adhesive (I used 3M brand), and cut out the shape with a band saw.

Use a compass to mark for the carving of the top. I opened the compass about ³⁄₈" between the pencil and point and formed the line by holding the steel end flush with the table edge as the compass traveled around the perimeter of the top.

Use a rasp to remove band saw marks from the edges. I used two hand screws to hold the tabletop firmly to the workbench.

Use a straight-cut bit in the router to freehand a relief cut prior to hand carving.

Use a shallow-radius gouge to cut along the pencil line. I cut to the same depth as the routed channel.

Use the shallow gouge to shape the transition from the flat plane of the top to the routed channel.

10 Use a random-orbit sander to remove the chisel cuts, or use extreme patience and care to organize your cuts and allow them to be part of the pattern of the top.

11 Use a roundover bit in the router to shape the underside of the tabletop.

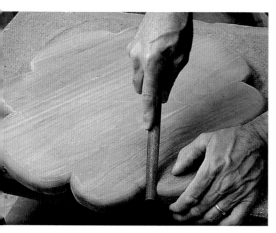

12 Use a rasp to finish shaping the underside of the tabletop, cutting in where the router can't reach.

13 To begin making the post, start by cutting it to size on the band saw. My piece of walnut had a great deal of sapwood to cut away and knots to consider. After jointing and planing the post to its final dimensions, use the table saw with the arbor tilted to 30° to cut the post stock to shape. Note that the post is cut from 2½" x 2⅞" stock.

14 To begin making the jig for cutting the tapered dovetails, taper stock on a jointer. Place one end beyond the cutter. As the stock passes over the jointer, it becomes tapered toward the opposite end. Note that the guard is pulled back for a clear view of the operation and the machine is off in this photograph. Use of guards and push blocks is recommended for safety.

15 Use a brad nailer to build a template around the tapered piece. This is done log-cabin style with corners overlapping and nailed to capture the shape of the interior piece.

16 To complete the jig for routing the tapered dovetail, add a block to the underside, with a screw hole positioned to meet the center of the post. Use a screw to secure one end of the jig to the post and a clamp to hold the other in place.

17 Use a router, guide bushing and 15° dovetail bit to route the tapered dovetail channels in the column. A stop-block held in place by clamps controls the length of cut.

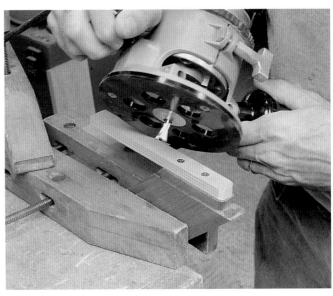

18 With the post mounted in a lathe, turn the desired shape. Then sand the post before removing it from the lathe. Start with 100 grit and work your way to 320. This is a great way to use old sanding belts and scrap sandpaper. Here you see the finished post after sanding.

19 To form the matching dovetail shape in the legs and upper table supports, attach the tapered dovetail form to the wood parts with screws. Getting just the right fit will take some trial and error working with scrap. The guide bushing in the router base allows the cutter to follow the template shape. Cut away from the narrow end of the taper to get a tighter fit.

20 After assembling the table post, legs and upper supports, sketch the shape on one part. After it's cut, this part becomes the model for marking and cutting the rest.

21 Use a disc sander to shape the outside edges of the table parts.

22 Use the end of a 6" x 48" belt sander to shape the inside curves.

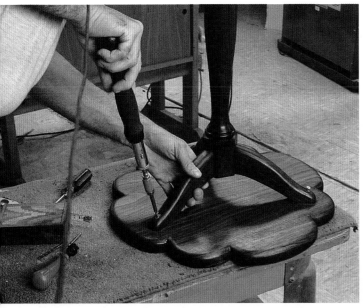

23 After sanding and applying a finish of Danish oil, use countersunk brass screws to attach the table base to the top.

A MEANINGFUL LIFE

My small town of Eureka Springs was founded at the site of a legendary spring. Some believed that the Basin Spring, preserved in a downtown park, was the original spring sought by Ponce de León as the Fountain of Youth. According to legend, the Basin Spring was a healing place used by American Indians who sought cures from disease and injury. The area around the spring was considered sacred ground and preserved by truce. In the late 1800s, it was "discovered" by settlers, and its wonders were proclaimed. Stories of miracles spread throughout the United States. Eureka Springs was founded in 1877 and grew rapidly to become one of the largest cities in turn-of-the-century Arkansas.

These days, Eureka Springs is a quaint tourist town with about 1,900 residents and several million tourists each year. The entire city is on the National Register of Historic Places, and unlike Colonial Williamsburg, which was created from scratch to promote an understanding of colonial America, Eureka Springs has been, from the moment of its founding, a Victorian community with a diverse population of interesting and unique individuals. Some people, marveling at the antics of our diverse population, have proclaimed: "Eureka, where the misfits fit." In my own view, however, we are not misfits but a collection of strong individuals seeking more meaningful lives and relationships.

It is impossible for me as a woodworker to view myself or my work as something apart from the community in which I live. Eureka Springs and its people inspire me and direct my work. Over the years, I've built display cabinets in classic Victorian style for local shops, doors for downtown buildings and a variety of furniture (including tables) for friends' homes. My first inlaid boxes were made for a local jeweler, and every other part of my woodworking life is a reflection of personal relationships.

There seems to be a need among artists of all kinds to find a niche — a theme that can be recognized in their work — so that it can be seen as different. The question I have learned to ask is not, "How can I make my work different?" but rather, "How can my work be meaningful?"

Being a woodworker in a small town with a diverse population and with a wide variety of tastes and interests has kept me challenged and inspired. The question, "How can I make my work meaningful?" has never been hard to answer. It is always as meaningful as personal friendship can make it.

Perhaps as the settlers, and the Native Americans before them, gathered at Basin Spring, the real healing was not in the water but in the spirit in which they gathered. And maybe today, the healing we seek can be found in the understanding and encouragement we offer each other as we seek meaning in our own lives. Somehow, it works for me.

dovetailed hall table

Over the years, I've seen many tables done by other furniture makers using dovetails to connect the sides to the top. This is my first. I chose to complicate my table by using angled legs and by making the top angled as well, giving it visual interest beyond the basic beauty of dovetails and wood. The two halves of the table form the sides of a river. Its open meander, penciled at random and intended to capture a sense of free-flowing spirit, allows light to pass through the top, re-creating its pattern in light and shadow on the lower shelf. The two sections that form the table are connected with sliding dovetail keys, which allow the sections to expand and contract independently in response to changes in relative humidity.

For me, this table was an exercise in design and playfulness. Beyond that, the pleasure and satisfaction one finds in cutting dovetails makes this a meaningful project. I chose cherry for this table because it is one of my favorite woods to work with. It ages to a deep red-brown color. Its quiet grain is easy to match for continuity throughout a piece of furniture, and it is a pleasure to cut with either power or hand tools.

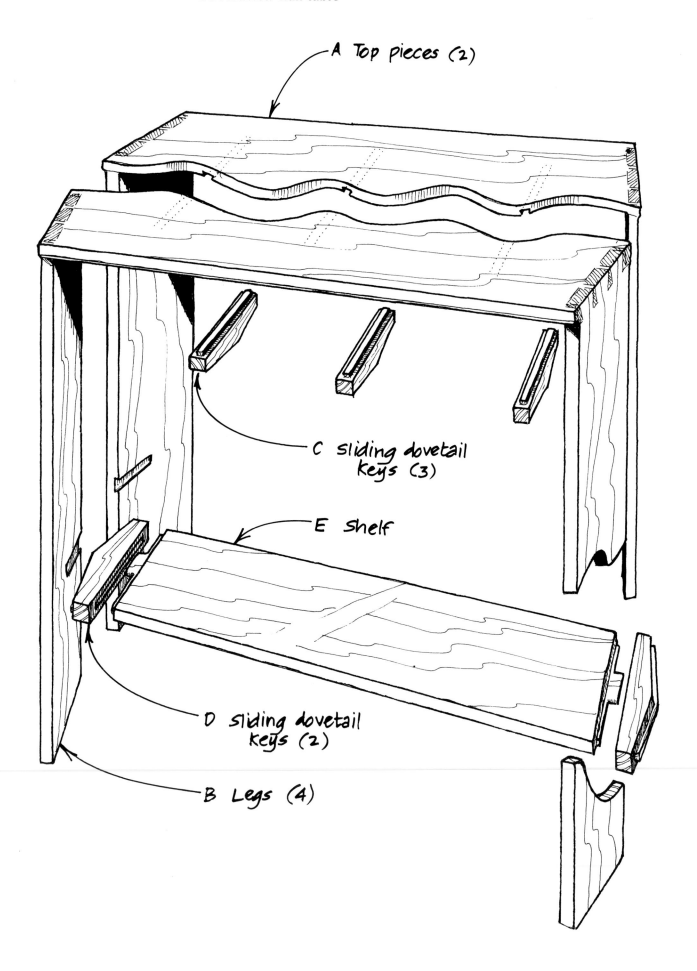

A Top pieces (2)

C Sliding dovetail keys (3)

E Shelf

D Sliding dovetail keys (2)

B Legs (4)

CUTTING LIST (INCHES) • dovetailed hall table

REF.	QTY.	PART	STOCK	THICKNESS	WIDTH	LENGTH	COMMENTS
A	2	Top pieces	Cherry	1	$7\frac{1}{2}$	$42\frac{1}{2}$	Cut at 8° angle
B	4	Legs	Cherry	1	6	33	Cut at 1° angle
C	3	Dovetail keys for top	Cherry	$1\frac{1}{8}$	$1\frac{5}{8}$	10	
D	2	Dovetail keys for legs	Cherry	$1\frac{1}{8}$	$2\frac{1}{8}$	10	
E	1	Shelf	Cherry	1	$9\frac{1}{2}$	$38\frac{5}{8}$	Includes $\frac{3}{4}$" tenons at each end

Hardware and Supplies

	4	Steel furniture glides
		Danish oil

CUTTING LIST (MILLIMETERS) • dovetailed hall table

REF.	QTY.	PART	STOCK	THICKNESS	WIDTH	LENGTH	COMMENTS
A	2	Top pieces	Cherry	25	190	1080	Cut at 8° angle
B	4	Legs	Cherry	25	150	840	Cut at 1° angle
C	3	Dovetail keys for top	Cherry	30	40	250	
D	2	Dovetail keys for legs	Cherry	30	255	250	
E	1	Shelf	Cherry	25	240	980	Includes 19mm tenons at each end

Hardware and Supplies

	4	Steel furniture glides
		Danish oil

1 I made this table from a stack of 7"- and 8"-wide rough-sawn cherry boards, with one wider 9½" board for the lower shelf. I cut the wood to a little over the finished length prior to planing, watching carefully for splits and cracks and allowing for them in marking the length of my cuts.

2 After jointing, planing and ripping the material to size, use a miter slide on a table saw to cut the pieces to size and shape.

3 Use a marking gauge to lay out the area for the "meander" to be cut. A pencil marking gauge allows you to erase form lines prior to sanding.

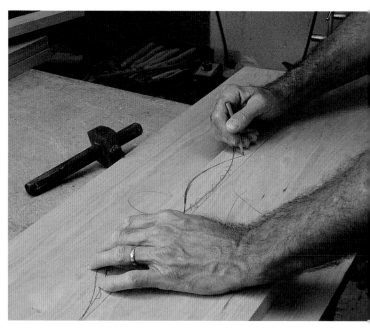

4 Mark the meander in pencil, being careful to keep the drawn line within the intended area.

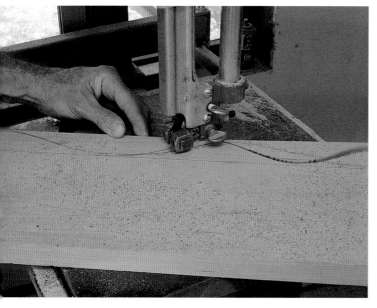

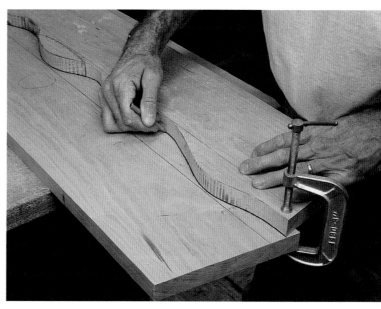

5 Use a band saw to cut the meander.

6 After cutting one side with a band saw, use that side to guide your pencil-marking on the opposite side.

7 Use the marking gauge to lay out the position for the dovetails on the top pieces and sides.

8 Lay out the dovetails on the legs. Use a sliding T-bevel and pencil to mark the shapes and positions of the tails. Use a small square to mark the cutting lines on the ends of the legs.

9 Use a dozuki saw or backsaw for cutting the tails.

10 A narrow chisel is used to cut away the space between the tails. I cut just shy of the line left by the marking gauge to allow for easy and more accurate cleanup when the bulk of the waste material is cleared away.

11 After cutting in from both sides, a small wedge can be lifted away.

12 With most of the waste material removed, use a wider chisel to clean up to the marking gauge line. This is an easy job: Allow the chisel to feel its way into place.

13 With a stop-block aligned to the dovetails that are cut in the legs, hold the top pieces in position for marking the shape of the pins. I use a small chip-carving knife to make the marks.

14 Use the dozuki saw to cut the pins.

15 Use a chisel to cut away the waste between the pins. Once again, make the first cuts away from the marking gauge line, allowing for a cleanup cut to be made after most of the stock is removed.

16 These dovetailed pieces are ready for final fitting and assembly.

17 Use a rasp to clean up the band-sawn edges of the top pieces.

18 Use coarse sandpaper to sand the edges, working gradually to finer grits.

19 To route for the sliding dovetail keys that hold the table together, make a routing jig. I use a log-cabin technique to build the jig with overlapping corners. The exact dimensions of the jig are dependent on the size of the router base, the width of cut desired and the length of cut planned.

20 To route the dovetail recesses in the legs, clamp them to the workbench top in the same angled relationship they will have in the finished table. Then proceed to route using the 15° dovetail cutter.

21 Before routing the sliding dovetail keys to fit the recesses, I make a test piece to make certain of the proper depth.

22 Before band sawing and routing the sliding dovetail, transfer the angle of the top to parts for connecting the base of the table. I use the sliding T-bevel, mark in pencil, band saw the shape and clean up the cut on the jointer.

23 Using a router table and dovetail router bit, route the dovetailed keys to fit.

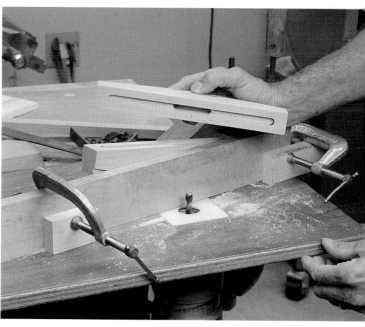

24 Test the fit of parts prior to assembly.

25 Use the router table to cut the mortises for the lower shelf to fit. I cut the long mortise first, using stop-blocks to control the length of cut. Raise the height of the cutter in small increments to avoid broken bits and unnecessary danger. Adjust the position of the stop-blocks to route the deeper center mortise.

26 To begin forming the lower shelf, first make a dado cut using the router on both sides of the shelf ends. This will form the stub tenon, which holds the shelf level in the supports.

27 With the board standing on end, as shown here, make cuts to begin forming the tenons.

28 Using a table saw and a fence, continue forming the tenons.

29 Waste around the tenons can be trimmed away using a sled on the table saw. Use a stop-block to accurately position the cut.

30 Use a band saw to cut away part of the tenon, leaving only a shoulder to fit in the shallow mortise and the longer tenon.

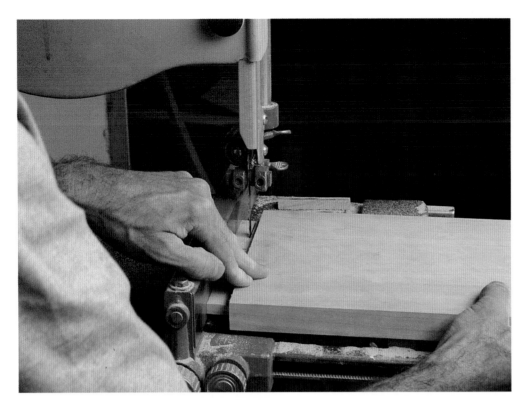

31 Use a rasp to round the corners of the tenons to fit the mortises. Then use a low-angle block plane to shape and soften the edges of the table parts prior to sanding and assembly, as shown here.

32 Spread glue on the dovetails and pins prior to assembly.

33 A little gentle tapping will seat the dovetails tightly together.

34 The two halves of the table need to be assembled quickly and before the glue sets, allowing some flexibility in the dovetails for the angled parts to fit.

DESIGN AND MEANING

In the world of contemporary furniture and design, making tables is an "anything goes" proposition. American woodworkers have been cut loose from convention to explore their own creativity. Fresh designs stretch the limits of imagination, as shapes, materials and functionality converge. Woodworkers attempting to enter the world of furniture design may feel that they need to be unique in order to succeed and be noticed, and that good design involves being different. But there are limitations to this approach.

Functionality is often sacrificed to "flair" in work that struggles to be different. What may seem fresh at first sight may lose interest and appeal over time. Things made to surprise or shock the viewer may end up in attics or landfills when their lack of usefulness or meaning becomes clear. (I have to mention, however, that some of these things end up in museums, too!)

Good design can be drawn in part from the relationships we have with the people, tools and materials. What we make, and how we make it, describes our relationships with the world and with each other, and establishes meaning in our own lives.

In my work, function is my first concern. With customers I ask, "How will this be used, and what are your needs?" In designing furniture for my own home, my wife plays a very strong role, as we discuss the merits and fit of a number of designs before the first piece of wood is cut. Functionality in a bedside table means not only that it must hold a lamp at the right height to be useful to its owner but that it must "fit" the space and enhance the surroundings. These are concerns that can only be met through discussion with the persons for whom a table is made.

Each piece fills a function in the woodworker's life as well. Many times I choose to do projects for people in styles that are not of my interest because they present the opportunity to learn a new technique, cultivate a friendship or tell a story. To limit one's view of functionality to how well a table holds a lamp is to overlook the world of personal growth and to ignore the real motive that keeps us making sawdust: living more meaningful lives.

The surprising thing is that in using "meaning" as a guide to our work, it leads to personal expression that is both different and universal. In time, the unique meaning of our own lives becomes expressed in what we do with wood and has the power to touch others in ways that may offer deeper meaning in their lives, as well.

recycled redwood **deck table**

When we had some work done on the exterior of our home, the front porch had to be pulled off and replaced. The 20-year-old redwood was too badly scarred and decayed to reuse, so we replaced it with treated wood, which kept us from feeling responsible for further loss of the redwood forests. But since I am a pack rat at heart and have difficulty parting with things that I might later find useful, I cut the redwood into sections and stashed it under the barn for later use.

Outdoor furniture tends to be short-lived. The first outdoor table I made for our home was nailed together from old weather-beaten pine boards. It was strong and useful for a number of seasons and was beautiful in a rustic sort of way. When we moved from an old log cabin to our current home, the table was left and I made a new one of cypress. Despite being

made with mortise-and-tenon joints, the table began to come apart and to decay, after only about 12 years.

While pocket holes have been around for many years and used in making furniture of all kinds, for a long time they were of less interest to me than more traditional joinery methods. Making this table convinced me of their usefulness, particularly for those who don't have time to learn traditional techniques, in situations where the expendable nature of the piece doesn't justify finer work or for beginning woodworkers who can hardly wait to get started.

When the table was complete, my wife asked, "How long will it take to weather to that beautiful gray?" "I can do it today!" I replied. A very light spritzing of vinegar, with steel wool dissolved in it, "weathered" our table to an immediate gray. Be sure to test your solution on scrap pieces. I had to dilute my solution several times before using it on the finished table.

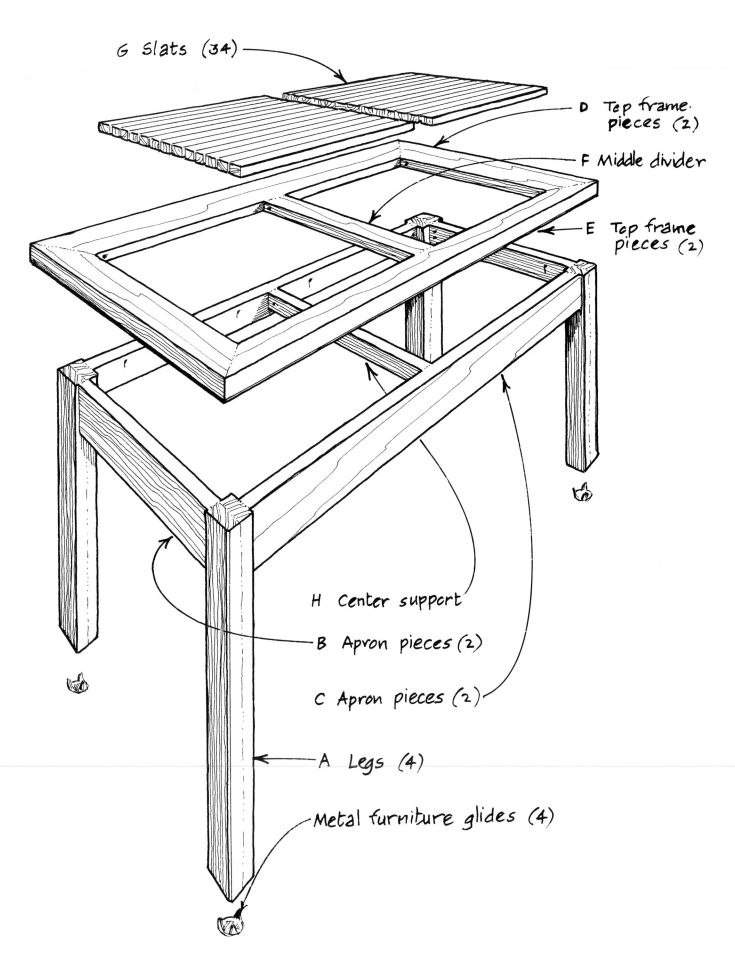

G Slats (34)

D Top frame pieces (2)

F Middle divider

E Top frame pieces (2)

H Center support

B Apron pieces (2)

C Apron pieces (2)

A Legs (4)

Metal furniture glides (4)

REF.	QTY.	PART	STOCK	THICKNESS	WIDTH	LENGTH	COMMENTS
A	4	Legs	Redwood	2	2	$28^{3}/_{4}$	Finished dimension
B	2	Short aprons	Redwood	$1^{1}/_{8}$	$3^{1}/_{4}$	$28^{1}/_{4}$	
C	2	Long aprons	Redwood	$1^{1}/_{8}$	$3^{1}/_{4}$	$54^{1}/_{2}$	
D	2	Short top frame pieces	Redwood	$1^{1}/_{8}$	$2^{1}/_{2}$	$33^{1}/_{2}$	
E	2	Long top frame pieces	Redwood	$1^{1}/_{8}$	$2^{1}/_{2}$	$59^{1}/_{2}$	
F	1	Middle divider	Redwood	$1^{1}/_{8}$	$2^{1}/_{2}$	$28^{1}/_{2}$	
G	34	Slats	Redwood	$1^{1}/_{8}$	$1^{1}/_{4}$	$26^{1}/_{8}$	To be arranged $1^{5}/_{8}$" between centers
H	1	Center support	Redwood	$1^{1}/_{8}$	$2^{3}/_{4}$	$29^{1}/_{2}$	

Hardware and Supplies

24	No. 8 x 2" screws
100 (approx.)	No. 8 x $1^{1}/_{4}$" screws
4	Metal furniture glides
	Polyurethane glue

REF.	QTY.	PART	STOCK	THICKNESS	WIDTH	LENGTH	COMMENTS
A	4	Legs	Redwood	50	50	730	Finished dimension
B	2	Short aprons	Redwood	30	80	720	
C	2	Long aprons	Redwood	30	80	1385	
D	2	Short top frame pieces	Redwood	30	65	850	
E	2	Long top frame pieces	Redwood	30	65	1510	
F	1	Middle divider	Redwood	30	65	720	
G	34	Slats	Redwood	30	32	663	To be arranged 41mm between centers
H	1	Center support	Redwood	30	70	752	

Hardware and Supplies

24	No. 8 x 50mm screws
100 (approx.)	No. 8 x 32mm screws
4	Metal furniture glides
	Polyurethane glue

2 For making the table legs, use polyurethane glue to laminate the material for the legs. I used 1⅛" stock. The polyurethane glue is applied to one side only and forms a waterproof bond.

1 Whenever you work with recycled wood, pay particular attention to all nails and remove them with a claw hammer or crowbar. And don't be discouraged by appearance. Even badly weathered boards will provide plenty of good wood when planed down. Examine the wood carefully for missed nails or embedded gravel, which could damage planer knives.

3 Clamp the table legs securely as the glue dries. I stack them together to reduce the number of clamps required.

4 To cut the tabletop slats to length, I tilt the saw blade to a 7½° angle and cut from each side. This provides a tapered end to fit a matching shape cut in the inside perimeter of the top. This technique prevents slats from twisting in place and prevents the creation of open places in which water might collect and introduce decay.

5 Use the miter sled on the table saw to cut the perimeter parts of the table to length.

6 The Kreg pocket-hole jig is fast and easy: Place stock in the jig with the underside against the face of the jig, so screws will be hidden from view. Drill the slats first.

7 Use a block plane to lightly chamfer the slats and other inside parts.

8 Mark the location of the slats on the middle divider, then use the divider to transfer the markings to the end pieces. Note the pocket holes drilled in the mitered corners. The slats are arranged $1\frac{5}{8}$" between centers, starting at the middle.

9 Use a marking gauge to mark the center points of the slats. These marks will be used to accurately align the slats to the pencil marks.

10 Put a dab of polyurethane glue at the end of the slat, clamp it in place and drive the screw home. I used weatherproof screws to avoid rust and decay. Note how the tapered ends of the slats fit the matching cuts in the perimeter of the top. This fit allows a single screw to hold the slats without twisting.

11 Drill the holes in the aprons that will be used to attach the aprons to the tabletop and legs.

12 Use a 45° chamfering bit in the router to rout the aprons and legs.

13 Use the router to chamfer the edges of the tabletop. I take a shallower cut on the top and a deeper one on the bottom. This makes the top appear slightly lighter in weight.

14 Here's a simple trick: Use blocking to build the thickness of the apron and position it in relation to the leg. The block on the outside is ¼" thick, and the one on the inside is ⅝". This builds the 1⅛"-thick apron up to 2", the same thickness as the legs.

15 Move the blocks and put the other apron in place. The clamp holds things in position while the screw is driven home. Once the aprons are in place, lay the tabletop upside down, place the base in position and drive the screws from the apron into the top. Use screws to attach the center support.

USING RECYCLED MATERIALS

Many woodworkers around the world are using materials obtained for free. Some salvage old pallets, shipping crates or construction debris, pulling nails and then planing and shaping old wood to new uses. Some woodworkers have become adept at intercepting trees, even branches of trees, from their home communities, preventing them from going to waste in landfills, and using products made from those trees to awaken a new and deeper understanding of our natural world. This process is often high adventure for the woodworkers involved and represents a refreshing level of environmental concern enmeshed with an admirable sense of thrift.

If you've ever driven through a supermarket parking lot and observed pallets covered with grease and grime, most often made of obscure and unidentifiable woods, you may know something of the challenge involved.

I am convinced that the value of work lies not only in the appearance and usefulness of the finished product but also in the integrity of the process. There is often greater challenge in making something from near nothing than in purchasing and then using fine and expensive raw materials.

The intent of the maker is a crucial ingredient in the value of work and one that is often overlooked in the marketplace where people may see only the visible form and not its underlying reality. There is the old expression: "Beauty is only skin deep." My own view is that beauty is more than what we can see with our eyes. We may ask ourselves, for example, if a table made from endangered woods, where loss of habitat is the hidden cost, is really all that beautiful. From this perspective, perhaps, a simple table lovingly reclaimed from the pallets at the neighborhood supermarket may take on a patina of warmth surpassing work done with finer woods.

The age in which we live requires adopting new frames of reference through which to view our work. To those who choose to make use of salvaged woods, I offer my deepest regards.

a tale of
two tables

One of the lessons a woodworker quickly learns is that things don't always work out the way we want or expect. I planned this project to be about making a twiggy table from a spalted maple board and some elm branches my wife and I stripped of bark and left to dry in my shop some years ago. A woodworker hopes that every project will lead somehow to the next, better one. In this case, the twiggy table turned out

OK, except for being rather wiggly. The materials were not available to start from scratch to make another, so I decided to make a different table, similar in concept but totally different in design. So, here are two tables in place of one: the twiggy table and the neo-rustic table.

The spalted maple boards had been in my lumber collection for years. They were too beautiful to cut into inlay stock and too thin to resaw into book-matched door panels. They were carefully kept and admired until just the right use became known.

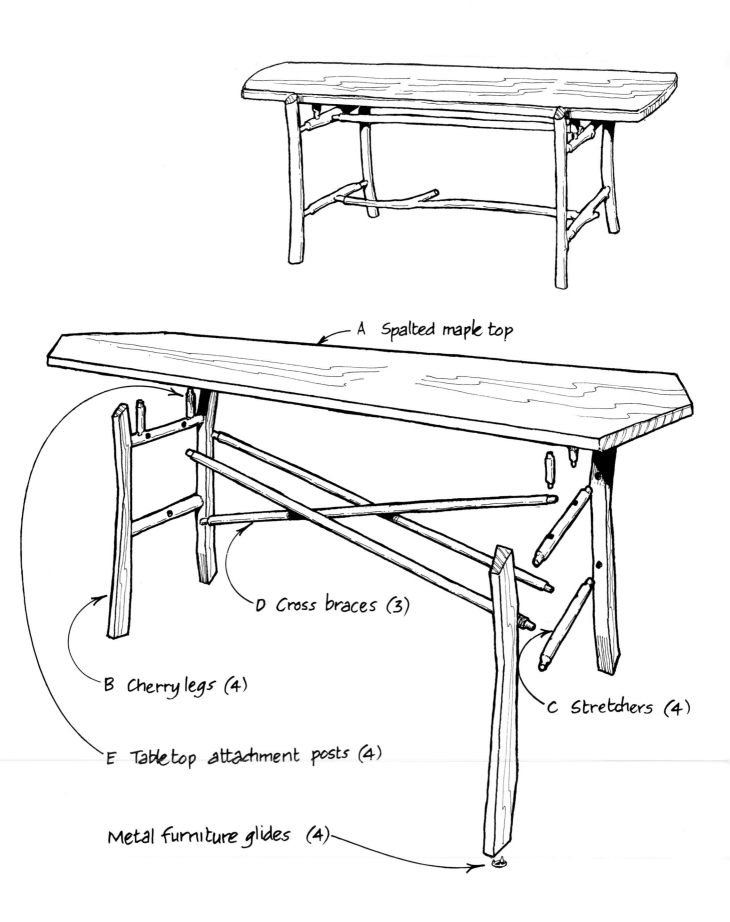

A   Spalted maple top

D Cross braces (3)

B Cherry legs (4)

C Stretchers (4)

E Tabletop attachment posts (4)

Metal furniture glides (4)

CUTTING LIST (INCHES) • a tale of two tables

REF.	QTY.	PART	STOCK	THICKNESS	WIDTH	LENGTH	COMMENTS
A	1	Top	Your choice	$7/8$	11	42	Choose any beautiful wood
B	4	Legs	5/4 Cherry	$1\,1/8$	$2\,1/2$	$17\,7/8$	Other woods will work as well
C	4	Stretchers	Cherry	$1\,1/8$	$1\,1/8$	$12\,3/4$	Turned round from square stock (allow for waste at ends for lathe attachment — measurement includes $1\,1/8"$ tenons at each end)
D	3	Diagonal cross braces	Cherry	$7/8$	$7/8$	$27\,1/2$	Turned round from square stock (allow for waste at ends for lathe attachment — measurement includes 1" tenon at each end)
E	4	Top attachment posts	Cherry	$7/8$	$7/8$	$3\,3/8$	Turned round from square stock (measurement includes $1/2" \times 7/8"$ tenon at each end)

Hardware and Supplies

	4	Metal furniture glides
		Polyurethane glue

CUTTING LIST (MILLIMETERS) • a tale of two tables

REF.	QTY.	PART	STOCK	THICKNESS	WIDTH	LENGTH	COMMENTS
A	!	Top	Your choice	22	280	1070	Choose any beautiful wood
B	4	Legs	5/4 Cherry	30	65	455	Other woods will work as well
C	4	Stretchers	Cherry	30	30	325	Turned round from square stock (allow for waste at ends for lathe attachment — measurement includes 30mm tenons at each end)
D	3	Diagonal cross braces	Cherry	22	22	700	Turned round from square stock (allow for waste at ends for lathe attachment — measurement includes 25mm tenon at each end)
E	4	Top attachment posts	Cherry	22	22	85	Turned round from square stock (measurement includes 13mm x 22mm tenon at each end)

Hardware and Supplies

	4	Metal furniture glides
		Polyurethane glue

Building a Twiggy Table

After cutting table legs to length, drill for the cross bracing to fit. Clamping the workpiece firmly to the worktable will help.

My twiggy table is fun to make. Aside from the planer, table saw and band saw used to prepare and shape the top, this table is built using only a dozuki saw for cutting the branches to length, a ⅝" drill bit, a Veritas power tenon cutter and an electric drill. The power tenon cutter is designed to cut the round shouldered tenons used in twig furniture and adjusts for a perfect fit.

To make a twiggy table, you'll need five or six elm branches about 1¼" to 1½" in diameter. They can be straight or twisted. Forks and branches will add interest to the finished design. Peeling the bark from the branches must be done when the wood is fresh cut, and cutting in spring is best. It is amazing how smooth the twigs are without even sanding. For an even more natural look, of course, the bark can be left on, but removing the bark will keep insect damage to a minimum. Since twiggy tables are built free-form, no two will ever be exactly alike. For those preferring to work with hand tools, the Veritas tenon cutter also can be adapted for use with a brace, and as a humanitarian gesture, Lee Valley/Veritas packages its tenon cutters with brace and adapter for distribution as a crutch-making kit in poor and war-torn countries.

The tenon cutter must be adjusted for an exact fit. A few practice cuts will be required and will also give you a chance to get the feel of it. I also found it to cut more smoothly after applying a thin coat of paste wax to the working surface. A dowel inserted into the cutter provides a stopping point to control tenon length.

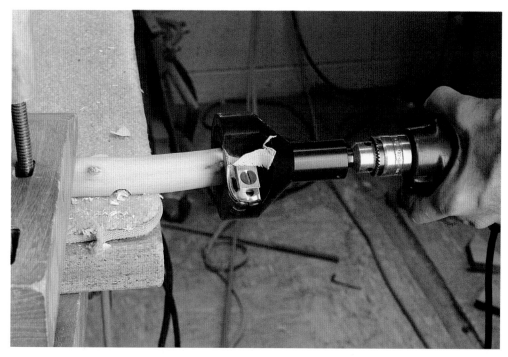

3 Clamp the workpiece very firmly before cutting the tenons. The power tenon cutter works quickly but exerts a great deal of force. The tenon cutter has a built-in level to assist in alignment. Carefully line up the drill and tenon cutter.

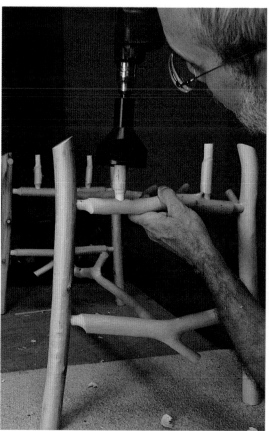

5 Drill holes in the underside of the top for attaching to the base. Check the depth carefully so as not to drill through. Before drilling, the locations for the holes were marked directly from the tenons on the base.

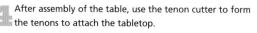

4 After assembly of the table, use the tenon cutter to form the tenons to attach the tabletop.

Building the Neo-Rustic Table

1 Use a band saw with the table tilted to a 15° angle to cut the ends to shape. The angles were laid out with a sliding T-bevel and marked in pencil after the wood was planed to thickness and cut to width.

This table is remarkably different in design from the twiggy table. While the twiggy table has a rustic appeal, this table has the clean lines associated with a more modern look. In the first table, the curved ends of the top reflect the round qualities of the branch material. In this second table, the angles provide a consistent theme throughout. The contrasting turned elements allow the use of round mortise-and-tenon joints, lending simplicity of assembly and fit.

2 Use a low-angle block plane to clean up the band saw marks. A sanding block could also be used.

3 Use the low-angle block plane to continue shaping the top. Plane a square edge, then lightly chamfer all the top edges to make them soft to the touch.

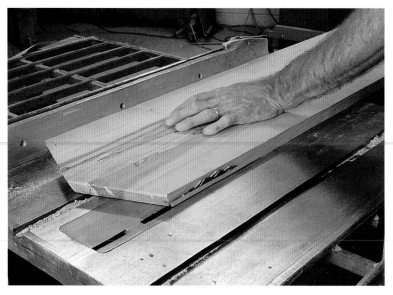

4 With your table saw tilted to a 15° angle, saw the sides of the tabletop to shape.

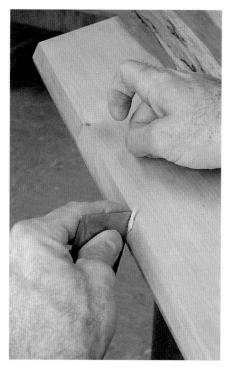

5 Use a cabinet scraper or sanding block to clean up the saw marks.

6 Use a square and pencil to mark the legs for the drilling of mortises.

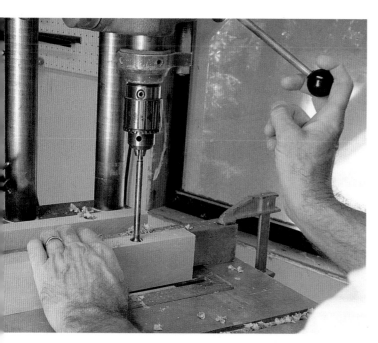

7 Use the drill press with fence to drill the ⅝"-diameter mortises. I drill them to a depth of 1".

8 Drill mortises in the cross stretchers. Note that this is done before they are turned on the lathe. A stop-block on the drill press fence is used here to position the hole.

9 To begin shaping the legs, make a 15° cut from each side. Note that this cut is planned to allow sufficient bearing surface against the table and fence.

10 Use a straightedge and pencil to mark the legs prior to shaping.

11 Use the band saw to cut the legs to shape. Keep the legs' remaining flat surfaces held securely to the table.

12 Using the miter slide on the table saw, trim the top ends of the legs to shape.

13 Use the stationary belt sander to remove the band saw marks.

14 A rasp is used to cut the areas the sander can't reach.

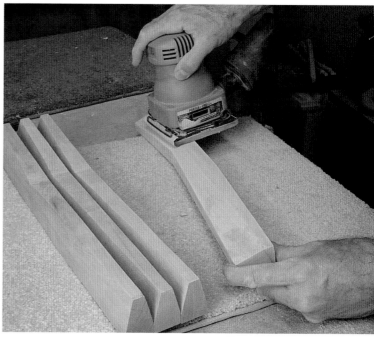

15 After cutting the legs to final shape, sand them smooth with the orbital sander. I use grits 150, 240 and 320.

16 Using the lathe, begin shaping the stretchers. Note the hole drilled for the diagonal stretchers to fit. I use a ⅝" open-end wrench to check for exact fit as the tenons are formed.

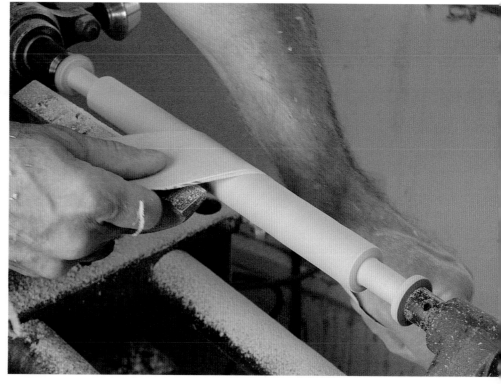

17 After the tenons are formed and the stretchers are turned round, sand them smooth while still on the lathe.

18 I used polyurethane glue to give a longer open time for assembly. It expands as it cures, so apply it sparingly to the insides of the mortises.

19 After the stretchers are in place and before they have time to dry, the diagonal stretchers must be glued in place.

20 As the table is assembled, use a square and tape measure to make sure everything is square and that the leg units are equal distances apart on both sides. This will be your last chance to make adjustments.

21 After the glue has had plenty of time to dry and can be safely handled, use a doweling jig to drill for the tabletop attachment pieces to fit. The Stanley doweling jig provides a depth stop for the drill to keep from going too deep. Careful marking and drilling at this point will make it easier to align and fit the tabletop.

22 Use the sled on the table saw to cut the top attachment pieces to length.

23 Use the drill press and ½" drill to make the holes for the tabletop attachment parts to fit.

WELCOME TO CHAOS

People visiting my shop often express amazement at the number of projects going on at once. Amidst parts for a desk and a table or two are boxes in various stages of completion, some children's rockers being carved prior to assembly, and more. I may have as many as five or six different projects going on at once: some in the design phase, some as rough lumber waiting to be planed, others awaiting assembly or final coats of finish. It can be confusing to the untrained eye, one not used to the chaos; but it is this chaos that can be fertile ground for an active imagination.

My working space consists of a two-car garage in which I do all the rough, dirty and dusty part of woodworking. I had it built with woodworking in mind, so it has a built-in dust collection system and is slightly wider and deeper than a normal garage. Across a small breezeway is my finish room, which is not often orderly but does offer a more dust-free environment for applying finishes and allowing them to dry. Next is my office, where I write, pay the bills and store boxes awaiting delivery to galleries. Because it's not necessarily good to have paperwork and creativity occupying one's mind at the same time (just ask the IRS about this one), I try to keep the office somewhat orderly; but it is a constant struggle.

My wife, Jean, calls my shop "the wilderness." Compared to the neatly arranged order of our home, things are indeed wild here. As someone who loves the outdoors, I have learned to take her remarks as a compliment.

It would seem that chaos could be a serious liability with regard to efficiency. It probably is. But as an artisan, whose moods and creative energies fluctuate in response to changes in the weather, personal events and even the national news, I have come to regard near-chaos as an ally in my creative process. Having a variety of things to choose from in my work allows me to apply myself consistently. At any given moment in my shop, I can choose to sand, plane, sharpen planer knives or chisels, figure out tough challenges, such as new techniques or complicated measurements, or just sweep up — depending on how I feel at the moment.

The creative process is not an experience that proceeds like clockwork or according to a fixed schedule. It comes in flashes and moments of awakening, and perhaps is best revealed when circumstances lead one to peer over the edge into the world of chaos.

In the past, I felt the need to apologize to visitors about my "mess." Then I discovered that orderly people were seldom expected to apologize for a lack of creativity. Now when I receive guests, without apology, I welcome them to Chaos.

stone-topped hall table

Much of Eureka Springs was built with our native limestone. Many miles of stone retaining walls line our streets, form the foundations of our Victorian homes and create terraces in backyards. Our Carnegie Public Library and our world-famous hotels are made of limestone. While limestone is often thought of as a rough building material, it also can be polished smooth to the touch and can include natural forms and patterns appealing to the eye. The stone used in this piece has quartz crystal formations, bits of iron that give it red spots and a natural vein of darker color. It came from the limestone quarry that provided much of the stone for building Eureka Springs. Stone workers at the quarry cut it from a large block of stone and polished it to reveal its beauty.

The angles of this piece make it a challenge for a beginner. The first thing a person needs to know in making a table like this is to use the cutting list as a rough guideline for finished dimensions. Compare and recalculate the actual measurements as the piece progresses. In making this table, I worked from the same template used by the stone craftsmen for cutting the top. I carefully laid out the posts and aprons, the locations of the mortises and tenons on the template, but I knew that very small changes in cut can create the need to adjust other dimensions as the table evolves.

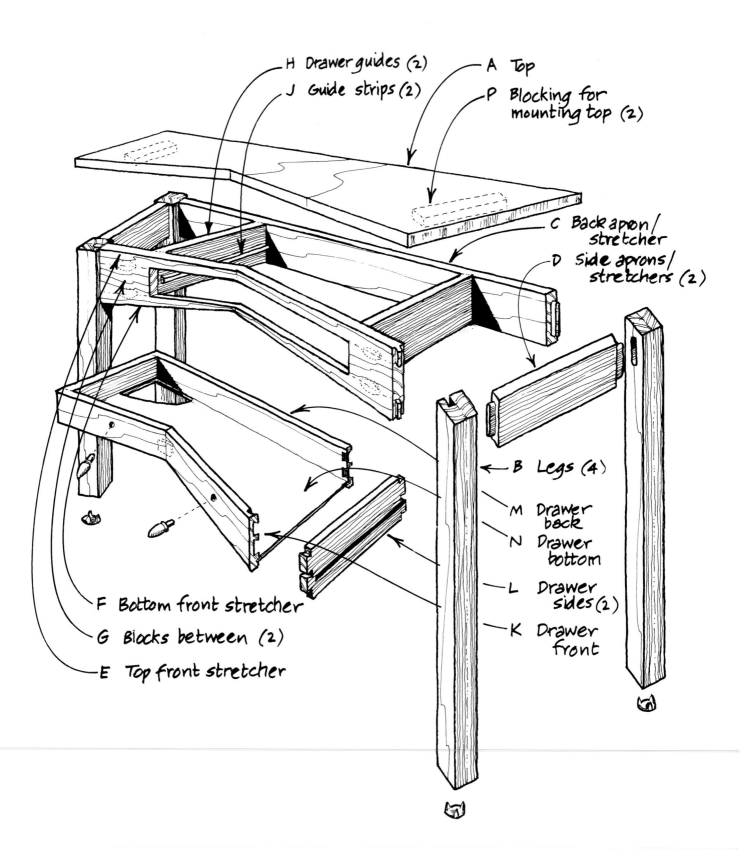

H Drawer guides (2)
J Guide strips (2)
A Top
P Blocking for mounting top (2)
C Back apron/stretcher
D Side aprons/stretchers (2)
B Legs (4)
M Drawer back
N Drawer bottom
L Drawer sides (2)
K Drawer front
F Bottom front stretcher
G Blocks between (2)
E Top front stretcher

CUTTING LIST (INCHES) • *stone-topped hall table*

REF.	QTY.	PART	STOCK	THICKNESS	WIDTH	LENGTH	COMMENTS
	1	Template	Masonite	$1/8$	$13^{5}/8$	42	
A	1	Top	Limestone		$13^{5}/8$	42	Have supplier shape based on template
B	4	Legs	Cherry	$1^{9}/16$	$1^{9}/16$	$30^{1}/2$	Glued up from $7/8"$ stock
C	1	Back apron/stretcher	Cherry	$7/8$	$3^{7}/8$	$38^{5}/8$	Includes $3/4"$ angled tenons at each end
D	2	Side aprons/stretchers	Cherry	$7/8$	$3^{7}/8$	$11^{3}/8$	Includes $3/4"$ tenons at each end
E	1	Top front stretcher	Cherry	$7/8$	2	$29^{1}/2$	Includes $3/4"$ angled tenons at each end
F	1	Bottom front stretcher	Cherry	$1^{1}/16$	2	$29^{1}/2$	Includes $3/4"$ angled tenons at each end
G	2	Blocks	Cherry	$3/4$	$2^{1}/2$	$2^{3}/4$	
H	2	Drawer guides	Cherry	$3/4$	$2^{1}/2$	$10^{1}/2$ $^{+}/_{-}$	Includes $1/2"$ tenon at each end
J	2	Guide strips	Cherry	$1/2$	$1/2$	$9^{1}/2$	Approximate dimensions
K	1	Drawer front	Cherry	$3/4$	$2^{1}/2$	22	Cut from rough stock
L	2	Drawer sides	Cherry	$5/8$	$2^{7}/16$	$9^{15}/16$	
M	1	Drawer back	Cherry	$5/8$	$2^{7}/16$	$21^{1}/8$	
N	1	Drawer bottom	Cherry	$1/4$	$9^{7}/16$	$20^{3}/8$	Trace for shape and cut to fit
P	2	Blocking	Cherry	$3/4$	$1^{1}/2$	$9^{13}/16$	For mounting top

Hardware & Supplies

	4	Steel furniture glides
	4	Biscuits

Note: All the sizes shown are approximate and will have to be adjusted to allow for changes in angle.

CUTTING LIST (MILLIMETERS) • *stone-topped hall table*

REF.	QTY.	PART	STOCK	THICKNESS	WIDTH	LENGTH	COMMENTS
	1	Template	Masonite	3	350	1070	
A	1	Top	Limestone		350	1070	Have supplier shape based on template
B	4	Legs	Cherry	40	40	775	Glued up from 22mm stock
C	1	Back apron/stretcher	Cherry	22	125	980	Includes 19mm angled tenons at each end
D	2	Side aprons/stretchers	Cherry	22	125	290	Includes 19mm tenons at each end
E	1	Top front stretcher	Cherry	22	50	750	Includes 19mm angled tenons at each end
F	1	Bottom front stretcher	Cherry	27	50	750	Includes 19mm angled tenons at each end
G	2	Blocks	Cherry	19	65	70	
H	2	Drawer guides	Cherry	19	65	265 $^{+}/_{-}$	Includes 13mm tenon at each end
J	2	Guide strips	Cherry	13	13	240	Approximate dimensions
K	1	Drawer front	Cherry	19	65	560	
L	2	Drawer sides	Cherry	16	63	253	
M	1	Drawer back	Cherry	16	63	535	
N	1	Drawer bottom	Cherry	6	240	518	Trace for shape and cut to fit
P	2	Blocking	Cherry	19	38	250	For mounting top

Hardware & Supplies

	4	Steel furniture glides
	4	Biscuits

Note: All the sizes shown are approximate and will have to be adjusted to allow for changes in angle.

1 Use Masonite as template material, a pencil, a marking gauge and a steel square to lay out the location of the legs, aprons, mortises and tenons. When the template was complete, I turned it over to the stone workers and waited until the finished top was complete before proceeding with the next steps.

2 To form the legs, either use 8/4 stock or carefully match grain patterns in thinner stock. I use the triangle marks to help in realigning the wood as it is glued.

3 I use fingers to spread the glue. It's messy, but no one will say I'm not involved in my work.

4 A bit of glue squeezed out between the boards is a sign that the glue has been well-distributed and amply applied.

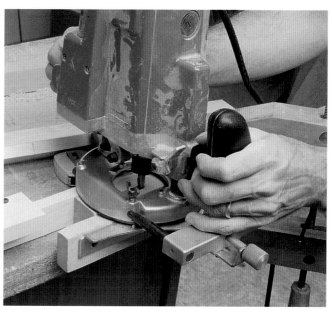

5 After jointing and planing the legs square and to dimension, carefully lay out the locations for the mortises. A centerline will help position the plunge router mortising jig. (See "Making Mortises with a Plunge Router" on page 74 to learn how to make this jig.)

6 Using the fence on the router to control the position of the cut and the jig to control the length of the finished mortise, rout the mortise in increments. Move the router back and forth between the stop-blocks of the jig as it is lowered into the cut.

7 This shows the completed mortise. The spiral ³⁄₈" cutter gives a smooth cut.

8 Use the template to guide cutting the front and rear aprons to the correct angle. The sliding T-bevel is used to transfer the angle from the template to the table saw for making the cuts.

9 Cutting the angled tenons is complicated, and requires that you use a variety of setups as shown in these four photos. Reverse the angle of the miter slide for cutting opposite sides.

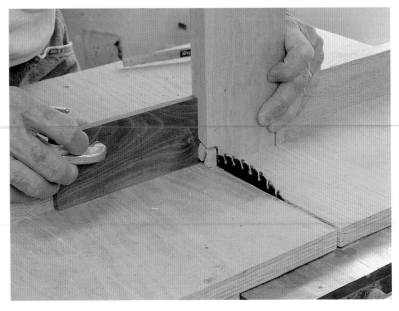

11 The router table is used to make the next cut in forming the tenons for the front stretchers. Use a straight-cut router bit with the fence to control the cut.

10 To begin forming the tenons on the front stretcher parts, make relief cuts on the table saw as shown. The angled stop-block is a cutoff from forming the part and is now useful in positioning the stretcher for further cuts.

12 Follow the sequence shown in these three photos for making the next cuts. The angled stop-block continues to be useful in positioning the workpiece.

13 A few quick swipes with a rasp will round the shoulders of the tenons to fit the mortises. To make it easier, I file a 45° bevel first and then round it with a few additional strokes.

14 With the back and front stretchers in position, mark the front stretchers so they can be cut to correspond to the shape of the front of the template.

15 Band saw one front stretcher to shape, then use a straightedge clamped in place and a template-following router bit to clean up the band saw marks. Rout from the right to the left to prevent tear-out.

16 Use one front stretcher as a guide for marking and sawing its mate.

17 Use the band saw to shape the underside of the lower front stretcher. The slight angle will reflect the angled front in the overall design of the table and make it appear lighter despite the weight of the top.

18 With the legs and front and back stretchers in position on the template, you can now take careful measurements for the side stretchers. Add to the measured length the lengths of the tenons for each end.

19 After practicing with the angled tenons, the straight ones will be a snap.

20 With the table dry-assembled, mark the positions for the drawer guides to fit.

21 Also check the correct angle and length of the drawer front before it is assembled.

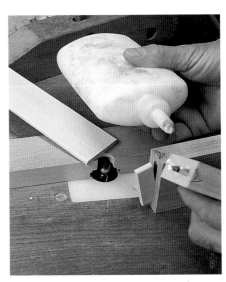

23 Use a roundover bit to form loose tenon stock, cut a piece to the required length and glue the two parts of the drawer front together.

22 To assemble the drawer front, first cut a ¼" mortise in the end of each half. I use a ¼" spiral bit in the router table and move the parts carefully between stops clamped to the top of the router table.

24 A bar clamp and a C-clamp are enough to pull the two halves together. Check the assembled drawer front before the glue sets by comparing it with the front stretchers of the dry-fitted table.

25 In making the drawer, first mark the tails using a pencil, marking gauge, sliding T-bevel and square, then with the drawer side held firmly in position, cut along the lines.

26 Use the dozuki saw to cut the lines that mark the tails.

27 Use a straight chisel to cut the waste from between the tails. I removed the outer waste using the table saw, sled and stop-block to position the cut.

28 In order to use square-cut dovetails on the angled drawer front, square the points where the sides fit the ends of the drawer front. This is done in a two-step process on the table saw.

30 To cut half-blind dovetails, the cut is made at an angle, leaving the balance to be carefully chiseled away. This task requires some practice. It is a job that gets easier as your confidence grows.

29 Mark the pins directly from the tails with a chip-carving knife. A block of wood clamped along the marking gauge line helps to accurately position the drawer side while the marks are inscribed.

31 Gradually remove the waste between the pins using a sharp chisel. For angled dovetails like these, a bit of trial-and-error fitting is required.

32 Here's how the dovetails fit together when correctly cut. Be patient and practice on scrap wood until you have the technique right.

33 Rout the drawer sides, front and back, for the drawer bottom to fit. I use a ¼" straight-cut bit for this task.

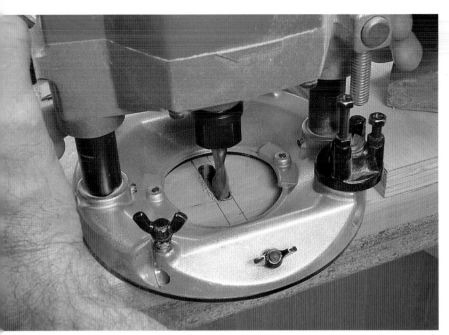

34 Rout the drawer sides and drawer supports using the plunge router. A guide piece will be glued in place on the drawer supports after routing. After routing the drawer supports, the tenons can be cut. Next, as shown here, use the plunge router to rout for the drawer guides to fit the front and rear aprons. I use a guide block clamped to the apron to guide the router travel and a stopping point sketched in pencil to control the length of cut.

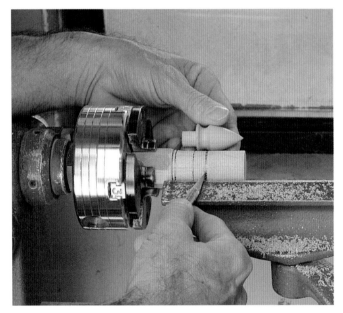

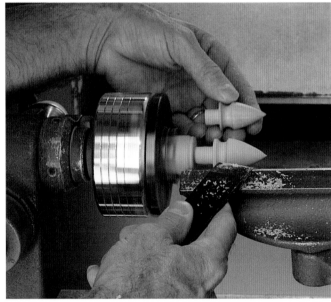

35 Make the drawer pulls from cherry. I turn one to completion, then use it as my guide in making the second. First mark out the dimensions using the first pull as the sample. Then shape and sand it on the lathe, as shown in these three photos.

THE EXPERIMENTAL NATURE OF WORK

The work I do with wood is nearly always experimental, though I'm careful not to tell my customers. Living in a small town and responding to a diverse clientele means that I am hardly ever asked to do the same thing twice, and if I were, by that time, I'd be in the midst of new interests and techniques, and it wouldn't turn out exactly the same, anyway. I don't know how many other woodworkers would feel comfortable living on the edge, not knowing with certainty before starting a project how it will turn out, whether or not the design will work, whether or not the finished project will meet the customer's needs and expectations. Perhaps to some degree or another, we are all on the edge. Our willingness to take chances by beginning projects is what keeps us growing as woodworkers.

The need for certainty about the outcome of one's work is one reason woodworkers look for plans, and perhaps a reason why one would read this book. But in my own work, plans are most often a very brief sketch. The details evolve over the course of each project. This is the case with many furniture makers. Thomas Moser, for example, mentions that he builds furniture before drawing the plans for it. The tables in this book were made first and drawn later. There are so many fine details that are difficult to put on paper and even harder to visualize in a drawing. Most often, the details can wait until later.

Over a period of time, confidence comes. The woodworker using premade plans finds that they must be changed to allow for variations in size and material or to allow for the use of tools or techniques in place of those suggested. After a period of frustration with such things, the artist may feel inspired to just wing it! Doodle on a board, build a model out of cardboard boxes to test the scale and then start cutting. It is a liberating thing to fly by the seat of the pants, to feel one's own creative spirit, to look down and see how far the fall of failure can be and then to bounce in for a safe landing.

I built desks and a storage unit in the office of my friend Bill, who plays a lot of racquetball. We discovered as I was installing my work that the carpenter remodeling the office had lowered the ceiling more than expected and my cabinets would not fit exactly as planned. We scratched our heads in frustration and worried, "How the heck can we do this?" Then it came to me — one cut and one more set of hinges will make it work! Bill's response, typical of racquetball, was, "Good save!"

Landings aren't always safe. Sometimes they're bumpy and frightening. But they are the price we pay for flight.

36 Use construction adhesive on wooden blocks to secure the tabletop in position. When glued to the limestone top, the blocks will allow it to be removed as needed but will keep it from sliding as the table is in use.

glass-topped
conference table

This small glass-topped conference table, made from sugar maple and trimmed in black walnut, was made for the office of the director of the Greater Little Rock Area Chamber of Commerce. The challenge for me was to design a table, a matching desk and a credenza that reflected the building design and the character and the interests of the director, a good friend, Paul Harvel. The building is constructed of glass and stainless steel and overlooks the Arkansas River in Little Rock. Because the table would be visible from the lower level of the building and from the office area on the second floor, I wanted the top to be glass and the structure of the table to be open and light so as not to obstruct vision.

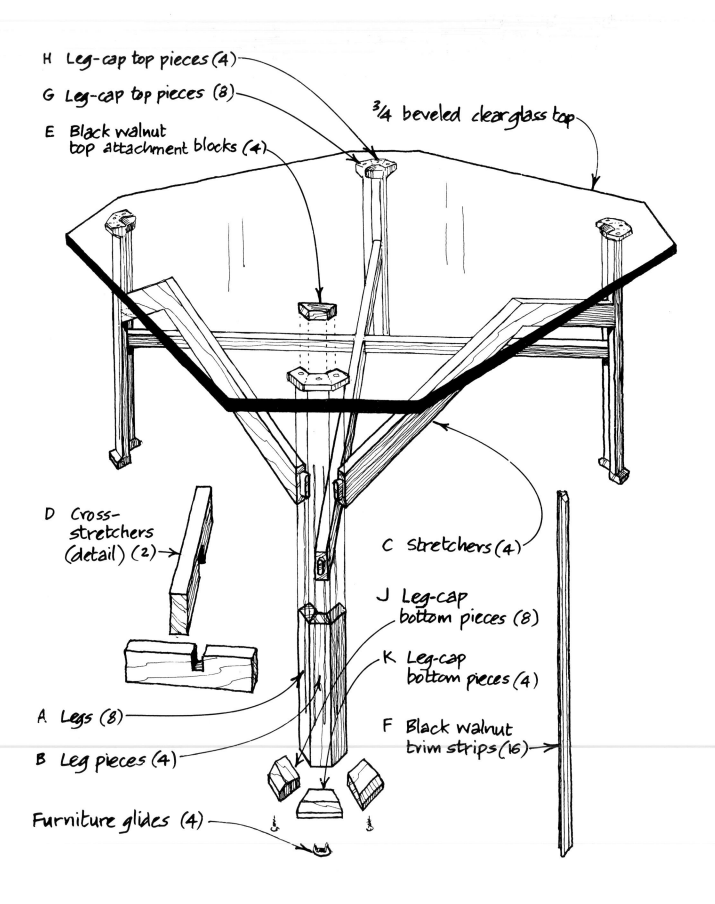

H Leg-cap top pieces (4)

G Leg-cap top pieces (8)

E Black walnut top attachment blocks (4)

¾ beveled clearglass top

D Cross-stretchers (detail) (2)

C Stretchers (4)

J Leg-cap bottom pieces (8)

K Leg-cap bottom pieces (4)

A Legs (8)

B Leg pieces (4)

F Black walnut trim strips (16)

Furniture glides (4)

CUTTING LIST (INCHES) • *glass-topped conference table*

REF.	QTY.	PART	STOCK	THICKNESS	WIDTH	LENGTH	COMMENTS
A	8	Leg pieces	Sugar maple	$7/8$	2	$26^5/_8$	Cut and sand to profile as shown in illustration
B	4	Leg pieces	Sugar maple	$7/8$	$7/8$	$26^5/_8$	
C	4	Stretchers	Sugar maple	$7/8$	$4^1/_2$	$25^1/_2$	Includes $1^1/_4$"-long tenons on ends
D	2	Cross stretchers	Sugar maple	$7/8$	1	$39^1/_2$	Includes $3/4$"-long tenons (leave these parts long and take actual measurements from the trial-assembled table)
E	4	Top attachment blocks	Black walnut	$3/4$	$1^1/_4$	$2^1/_2$	
F	16	Trim strips	Black walnut	$3/16$	$1/4$	$21^1/_2$	With $1/8$" x $1/8$" tenon, 21" long

Leg Caps

REF.	QTY.	PART	STOCK	THICKNESS	WIDTH	LENGTH	COMMENTS
G	8	Top pieces	Sugar maple	$3/4$	$1^3/_4$	2	These have a $22^1/_2°$ angle at one end
H	4	Top pieces	Sugar maple	$3/4$	$1^3/_4$	$2^1/_2$	These have a $22^1/_2°$ angle at each end
J	8	Bottom pieces	Sugar maple	$3/4$	$1^3/_4$	2	These have a $22^1/_2°$ angle at one end
K	4	Bottom pieces	Sugar maple	$3/4$	$1^3/_4$	$2^1/_2$	These have a $22^1/_2°$ angle at each end

Hardware & Supplies

	4	Metal tack-on furniture glides
	4	No. 6 x $1^1/_4$" screws (for securing leg caps to table legs)
	4	$3/8$" maple plugs (for concealing the screws that attach the leg caps)
	4	No. 20 biscuits
	1	$3/4$" beveled clear glass top (with corners cut 7" in from original corners)

CUTTING LIST (MILLIMETERS) • *glass-topped conference table*

REF.	QTY.	PART	STOCK	THICKNESS	WIDTH	LENGTH	COMMENTS
A	8	Leg pieces	Sugar maple	22	50	675	Cut and sand to profile as shown in illustration
B	4	Leg pieces	Sugar maple	22	22	675	
C	4	Stretchers	Sugar maple	22	115	650	Includes 32mm-long tenons on ends
D	2	Cross stretchers	Sugar maple	22	25	1005	Includes 19mm-long tenons (leave these parts long and take actual measurements from the trial-assembled table)
E	4	Top attachment blocks	Black walnut	19	32	65	
F	16	Trim strips	Black walnut	5	6	545	With 3mm x 3mm tenon, 535mm long

Leg Caps

REF.	QTY.	PART	STOCK	THICKNESS	WIDTH	LENGTH	COMMENTS
G	8	Top pieces	Sugar maple	19	45	51	These have a $22^1/_2°$ angle at one end
H	4	Top pieces	Sugar maple	19	45	64	These have a $22^1/_2°$ angle at each end
J	8	Bottom pieces	Sugar maple	19	45	51	These have a $22^1/_2°$ angle at one end
K	4	Bottom pieces	Sugar maple	19	45	64	These have a $22^1/_2°$ angle at each end

Hardware & Supplies

	4	Metal tack-on furniture glides
	4	No. 6 x 32mm screws (for securing leg caps to table legs)
	4	10mm maple plugs (for concealing the screws that attach the leg caps)
	4	No. 20 biscuits
	1	20mm beveled clear glass top (with corners cut 180mm in from original corners)

MAKING MORTISES WITH A PLUNGE ROUTER

Routing mortises with a plunge router is easy using a shop-made router jig. The router fence controls the position of cut, the router depth controls the depth of the mortise and the space between the blocks controls the length of the mortise.

The stop-blocks can be attached with screws or nails, and the jig can be discarded when the project is complete or kept for another project.

To make the jig, first measure the width of the router base, then subtract the width of the cutter and lastly add the desired length of the mortise. This measurement will give the appropriate distance between blocks. I mark the center between blocks to assist in aligning the workpiece for accurate location of the mortise.

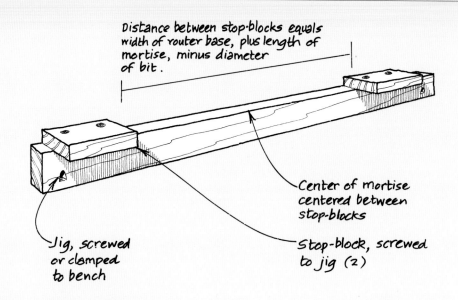

Distance between stop-blocks equals width of router base, plus length of mortise, minus diameter of bit.

Center of mortise centered between stop-blocks

Jig, screwed or clamped to bench

Stop-block, screwed to jig (2)

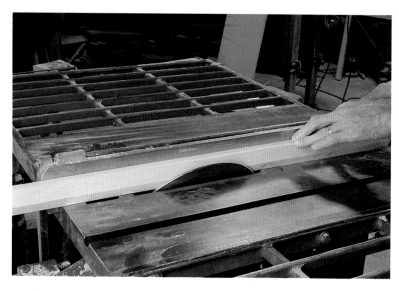

1 After cutting the leg pieces to shape, use a sanding disc in the table saw to remove saw marks. The sanding disc will prepare the surface more accurately for gluing than the saw will.

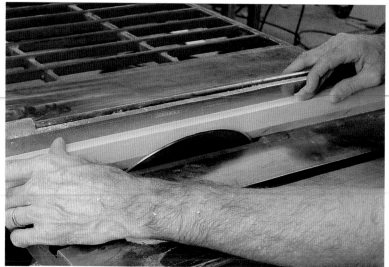

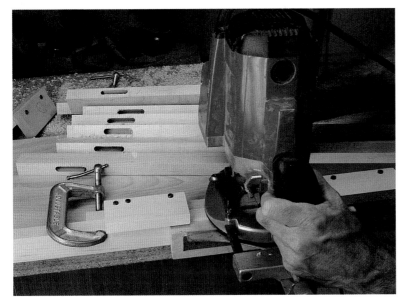

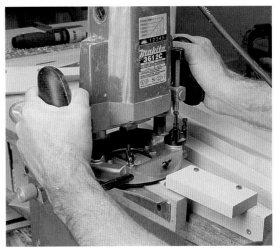

3 To use the jig, set the router depth to the desired mortise depth and gradually lower the router into the cut in shallow steps as it moves between stops.

2 Use the plunge router mortising jig to rout the mortises in the leg parts prior to gluing. This jig was made to cut 2½"-long mortises.

4 Use the plunge router mortising jig to rout for the cross stretcher to fit. I built this jig to make 1" mortises.

5 I use biscuits to align the leg parts for gluing. After spreading the glue, use package-sealing tape to wrap the parts tightly in position. Note the assembled legs in the background.

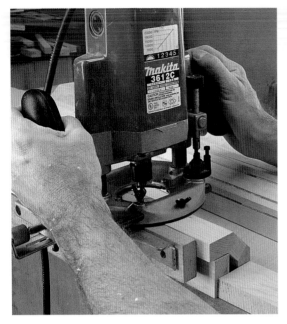

6 Use the plunge router with a ⅛" straight-cut bit to rout for the walnut trim to fit the legs. Note the blocking used to hold the leg for routing.

7 To form the tenons on the aprons, I use a shop-made tenon-cutting jig on the table saw. Make the first cuts with the stock standing up. Index both cuts from the same side for increased accuracy.

8 Use the sled on the table saw for the next cuts. Raise the blade just high enough to touch the tenon. The stop-block clamped to the sled controls the length of the tenon.

9 Use the sled to position the cuts that form the top and bottom edges of the tenons. The tenoning jig on the table saw would also work well for this.

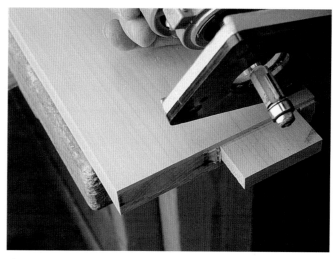

10 Use the band saw to cut away most of the remaining waste, then use a laminate trimmer with flush-cut bit to finish the cut as shown here. A sharp chisel will cut where the bit won't reach.

11 Use a pilotless 45° chamfering bit to rout the ends of the stretchers where they will fit the legs. The fence controls the position of the cut.

12 Use the band saw to cut the aprons to shape. I mark them out in pencil, cut just outside the line and finish with the router. A straightedge clamped in place guides the template-following router bit.

13 A few quick strokes with the rasp will round the corners of the tenons. I first rasp a 45° angle on each corner, then finish the round.

14 I use a 30° miter sled on the table saw to cut the parts for making the leg caps.

15 Use the router table to rout mortises in the blocks for making the leg caps. I use a ¼" straight-cut router bit raised to about ½" in height above the table. This allows the use of 1"-long tenon stock.

16 With glue spread in each mortise, the loose tenon is inserted to join the parts. Note the ⅛" roundover bit in the router table used to form the loose tenons.

17 Squeeze them together hand tight and wrap with package sealing tape. I glue them two parts at a time, allowing the first joints to dry before adding the third.

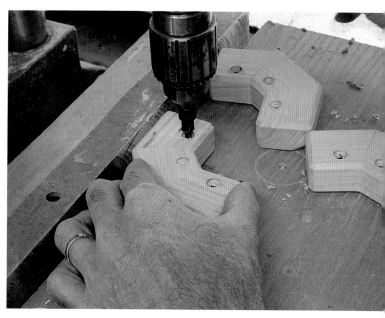

18 Use the drill press to drill the holes for mounting the leg caps with screws. I marked the locations for the holes in pencil. The fence controls the distance the hole is placed from the edge.

19 To begin forming the cross stretcher, cut overlapping dado joints in the ¾" x 1" stock.

20 After cutting the tenons on the ends of the cross stretchers, check the fit of the trial-assembled table.

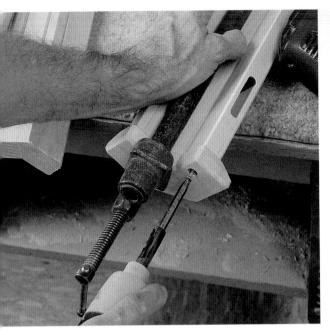

21 Use screws to secure the leg caps to the table legs. I use a clamp to hold the leg caps firmly in position while the pilot holes are drilled. Plug the screw holes with 3/8" maple plugs after they are screwed to the legs.

22 To allow plenty of open time on the gluing, I use polyurethane glue. It requires sparse use to keep from making a mess and should be applied to only one surface. I use a dowel to coat the insides of the mortises.

24 Use bar clamps to hold parts together while the glue dries. Use cardboard to keep the clamps from marring the wood.

23 Wiggle and push the parts together. The cross stretcher flexes slightly to allow assembly.

25 Form the walnut trim strips on the router table. I use a straight-cut router bit to form the tenon between two strips, then cut them apart and chamfer the edges with a 45° router bit. If you want to learn more about this technique, see one of my other books: *Simply Beautiful Boxes* or *Creating Beautiful Boxes with Inlay Techniques*.

26 Before installing the walnut trim strips, chamfer the ends to match the profile routed on the edges. I use a small straight chisel and a careful hand.

27 Glue the trim strips in place. Use a small glue bottle to put glue in the routed slot, then press the strip in place. If it is at all loose, use masking tape to hold it while the glue dries.

28 Use tack-on furniture glides. For hardwoods, I predrill the holes to keep from splitting the wood.

jean's cherry
dining table

Over the years I've made a number of pieces of furniture for our home. No single piece has been more anticipated and celebrated than our new dining table. My wife, Jean, is my toughest customer. While others may invite me to be more creative in my work, Jean says, "We're going to have this a long time, so it better be good!" She loves to be deeply involved in the planning. To get ideas, she pores over catalogs, clipping pictures of the things she likes, noting size and detail. Using cardboard, we make models of the space the piece will occupy so we can better imagine and visualize the finished piece. Laying out place mats helps to imagine where people will sit and how many will fit around the table at special dinners and celebrations.

Knowing that handmade chairs would require a very long wait, Jean ordered the chairs for our dining room from a catalog. To reflect the curves of the chair backs, I chose to cut curves in the table aprons. The cherry will age to a deep red-brown, in time contrasting the natural beech used in the chairs. The massive, straight legs are intended as counterpoints to the curved and slender lines.

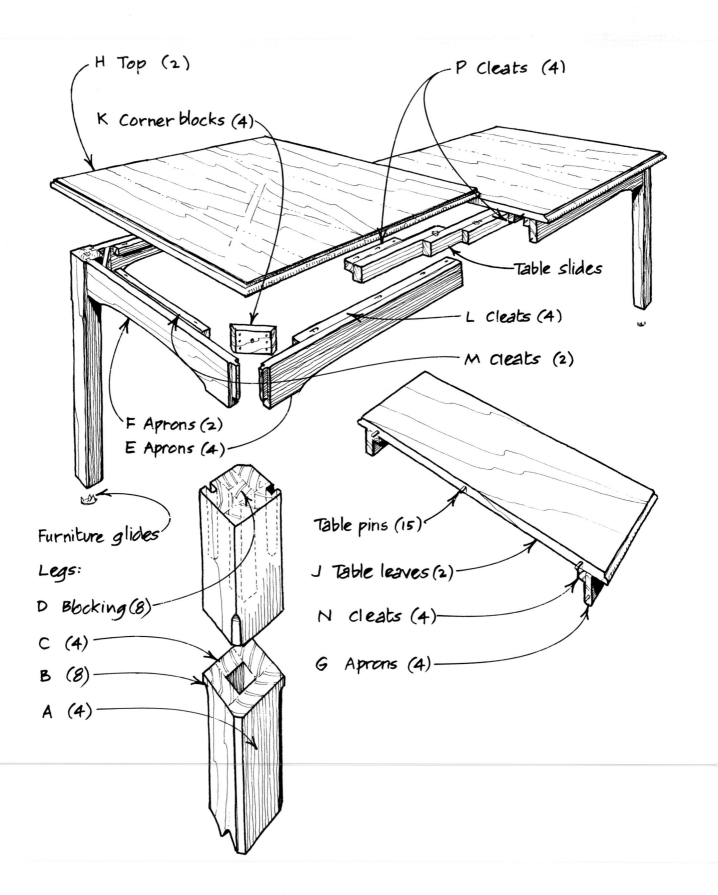

H Top (2)

K Corner blocks (4)

P Cleats (4)

Table slides

L Cleats (4)

M cleats (2)

F Aprons (2)

E Aprons (4)

Furniture glides

Legs:

D Blocking (8)

C (4)

B (8)

A (4)

Table pins (15)

J Table leaves (2)

N cleats (4)

G Aprons (4)

CUTTING LIST (INCHES) • jean's cherry dining table

REF.	QTY.	PART	STOCK	THICKNESS	WIDTH	LENGTH	COMMENTS
A	4	Leg pieces	Cherry	1	$2\frac{3}{4}$	29	
B	8	Leg pieces	Cherry	1	$1\frac{3}{4}$	29	
C	4	Leg pieces	Cherry	1	$\frac{3}{4}$	29	
D	8	Leg pieces	Cherry	$\frac{3}{4}$	$\frac{3}{4}$	5	Blocking at ends
E	4	Apron pieces	Cherry	$\frac{7}{8}$	$4\frac{1}{4}$	$23\frac{1}{8}$	
F	2	Apron pieces	Cherry	$\frac{7}{8}$	$4\frac{1}{4}$	$31\frac{1}{4}$	
G	4	Apron pieces	Cherry	$\frac{7}{8}$	$3\frac{1}{16}$	12	
H	2	Top pieces	Cherry	$\frac{7}{8}$	39	28	Cut from narrower 42"-long stock
J	2	Table leaf pieces	Cherry	$\frac{7}{8}$	12	39	Cut from narrower stock
K	4	Corner blocks	Cherry	$\frac{7}{8}$	$3\frac{3}{4}$	$6\frac{1}{4}$	
L	4	Cleats	Cherry	$\frac{7}{8}$	$1\frac{1}{8}$	20	
M	2	Cleats	Cherry	$\frac{7}{8}$	$1\frac{1}{8}$	24	
N	4	Cleats	Cherry	$\frac{7}{8}$	$1\frac{1}{8}$	$11\frac{7}{8}$	
P	4	Cleats	Cherry	$\frac{7}{8}$	$1\frac{1}{8}$	13	Attaches table slides to top

Hardware & Supplies

	72	No. 20 biscuits
	9	$\frac{3}{8}$"-diameter table pins
	4	$\frac{7}{8}$" steel three-prong furniture glides
	1 pr.	26" table slides
	72	No. 8 x $1\frac{1}{2}$" wood screws
	4	$\frac{5}{16}$" x $2\frac{1}{2}$" lag bolts with washers
		Danish oil

CUTTING LIST (MILLIMETERS) • *jean's cherry* dining table

REF.	QTY.	PART	STOCK	THICKNESS	WIDTH	LENGTH	COMMENTS
A	4	Leg pieces	Cherry	25	70	737	
B	8	Leg pieces	Cherry	25	45	737	
C	4	Leg pieces	Cherry	25	20	737	
D	8	Leg pieces	Cherry	20	20	130	Blocking at ends
E	4	Apron pieces	Cherry	22	108	587	
F	2	Apron pieces	Cherry	22	108	793	
G	4	Apron pieces	Cherry	22	78	305	
H	2	Top pieces	Cherry	22	990	710	Cut from narrower 1070mm-long stock
J	2	Table leaf pieces	Cherry	22	305	990	Cut from narrower stock
K	4	Corner blocks	Cherry	22	95	158	
L	4	Cleats	Cherry	22	29	508	
M	2	Cleats	Cherry	22	29	610	
N	4	Cleats	Cherry	22	29	300	
P	4	Cleats	Cherry	22	29	330	Attaches table slides to top

Hardware & Supplies

	72	No. 20 biscuits
	9	10mm-diameter table pins
	4	22mm steel three-prong furniture glides
	1 pr.	660mm table slides
	72	No. 8 x 38mm wood screws
	4	8mm x 64mm lag bolts with washers
		Danish oil

MAKING SOLID WOOD TABLETOPS

Solid wood expands and contracts with changes in relative humidity. Dealing with the shrinkage and expansion of wood is one challenge faced by woodworkers, and the cause of a great deal of disappointment for beginners. To add further complications, wood doesn't expand or contract evenly across its thickness or width. It is affected by shrinkage factors called *radial* and *tangential*. These factors differ in each species of wood, so as wood shrinks and expands, it has a tendency to warp slightly along the orientation of the annual rings (see arrows on drawing). This can cause wide tabletops to warp and cup.

Some woodworkers suggest all tabletop material be cut into 3"-wide strips and assembled randomly to overcome this natural tendency. Working with beautiful woods, I've never found the heart to rip wide pieces into narrow when the plan would allow for wide stock to be displayed in its natural beauty.

One strategy I use for my tables is reversing the orientation of the grain in every other board as each board is selected and aligned for forming a tabletop. I mark the planed stock with an X on the bark side and with an O on the heart side of the stock, carefully observing the end grain of each board. This will not eliminate all potential for cupping or warping but will reduce it to a manageable level in most cases.

I also try to make sure that both sides of the tabletop are finished to the same degree and with the same finishes. This keeps the tabletop breathing equally on both sides and helps avoid stresses caused by exposure to moist or dry conditions on one side only.

One of my early disappointments in table-making gave me a lesson to last a lifetime of woodworking. I had made a large inlaid oak table from kiln-dried wood. I had been told that "kiln-dried wood won't warp or shrink" (a lie perpetrated by wishful thinkers?). Who knew it could expand? I attached the top to the table base securely with screws, then discovered on a rainy day that it had warped like the hull of a huge watermelon as the top expanded against the tension of the screws and framework on the other side.

I learned from that lesson to keep my relationship with wood loose and trusting. A gentle hand in attaching tabletops with allowance for expansion and contraction is essential to design.

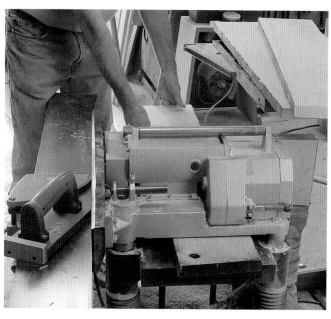

1 Select the cherry for the top first, saving that of lesser quality for less visible uses.

2 Plane the wood to thickness. I prefer to remove stock in small increments and watch the grain carefully to avoid tear-out.

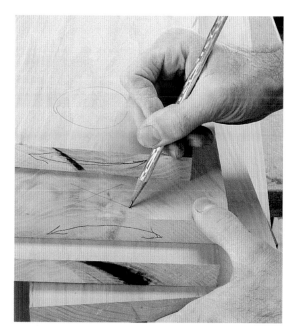

3 I mark the boards with an X on the bark side and O on the heart side. This allows me to limit possible cupping of the assembled tabletop. I've penciled lines on the ends of the boards to show orientation of the annual rings.

4 Lay the boards out X, O, X, O, etc., and mark lines for fitting biscuits between boards.

5 Biscuits are not required for the strength of the finished panel, but they do make alignment easy, reduce sanding time and create a flatter surface.

6 Spread glue on the boards. I lay a bead of glue and spread it with my fingers, taking care to squirt a bit into the biscuit slots.

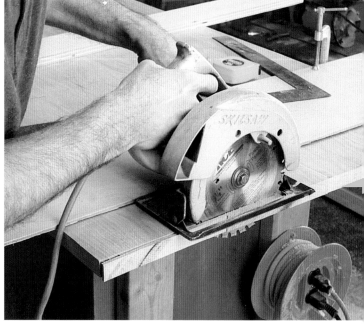

7 Putting clamps on both sides helps to keep the tabletop flat.

8 A guide fence clamped in place and a circular saw can be used to cut the top sections to length.

9 Use a belt sander and then a random-orbit sander to level the surface of the tabletop.

10 For routing the edges of the tabletop, clamp a piece of scrap wood where the router exits the cut. This prevents tear-out where the tabletop sections meet.

11 Rout the ends first, then the sides.

12 Use a curved sanding block to sand into the routed edge.

13 Use a doweling jig to drill holes for the table pins.

14 After the edges are sanded and the pinholes are drilled, the top gets its final orbital sanding.

15 To fabricate the legs, use biscuits to align the parts for gluing, as shown in these two photos.

16 Use bar clamps to hold parts together for the first gluing. All four legs are clamped together at once.

17 Finish the biscuiting and gluing of the legs, as shown in these two photos. Note the spacer blocks added to fill the ends of the legs.

18 Use the plunge router to rout for the table aprons to fit the legs.

19 Use a 45° chamfering bit to shape the legs.

20 Use a tenoning jig on the table saw to shape the tenons on the ends of the apron parts. Indexing the stock from the face side, I make the first cut then change the position of the fence for cutting the opposite side. Indexing both cuts with the same side against the body of the jig gives a good fit despite variations in the thickness of stock.

21 Finish cutting the tenon using a crosscut sled on the table saw, as shown in these two photos.

22 Use a chisel and rasp to finish shaping the tenon to fit the round shape of the mortise on the table legs, as shown in these two photos.

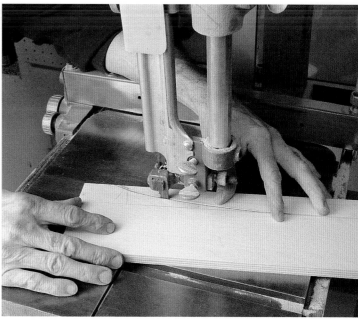

23 Use a marking gauge and pencil to mark the curve for the aprons on a piece of scrap birch plywood. I used the marking gauge for the straight part and sketched the balance by hand.

24 Band saw the birch plywood template to shape.

25 Use a rasp to smooth the template, removing the band saw marks and making a smooth, continuous curve.

26 Use the template to mark the aprons for cutting on the band saw.

27 After cutting on the band saw, a template-following router bit can be used to clean up the cut. Reposition the clamps to allow the full length of cut to be made.

28 Clamping all the aprons together gives a stable platform for belt sanding.

30 Carefully check the distance the screws will protrude into the tabletop.

29 Use the plunge router to rout expansion/contraction slots for pieces that attach the aprons and table slides to the tabletop. I first rout a ¼" slot, moving the router between pencil lines. After changing to a larger bit, rout for the washers and screws to fit.

31 Use a regular countersink at one end of the attachment parts. This end will fit where the aprons and tabletop halves meet at the center of the table.

32 Use biscuits to attach the parts to the table aprons and table slides, as shown in these two photos.

33 Glue the attachment blocks in place, and clamp the aprons and blocks together in pairs, as shown in these two photos.

34 Make corner blocks using the miter sled on the table saw.

35 Use screws to attach the corner blocks to the aprons, and use lag bolts with washers to attach the blocks to the table legs. I use a band clamp to hold the table parts together tightly while the corner blocks are put in place. Note that the Danish oil finish was applied prior to assembly.

36 Use screws to attach the top. The biscuits shown in the photo above are used as temporary spacers that allow room for the tabletop to expand during humid months.

37 Use screws to attach the table slide to the tabletop.

maple & elm
pedestal table

Pedestal-style tables are so easy to gather around, with no legs to interfere with placement of chairs. I made this one from elm and sugar maple, both natives of our Arkansas forest.

This table is built using the very simple technology of a shop-made cylinder lathe which, unlike other lathes, uses the router to remove stock while the cylinder is turned by hand into the cut. My cylinder lathe was made in an afternoon from leftover 2x4s, scrap plywood, hardwood strips and some V-belt pulleys and ½" bolts, which are used as axles for the pulleys and centers for mounting the cylinder to the lathe. I've used it to make cylinders for tables and turned quarter columns for architectural installations.

101

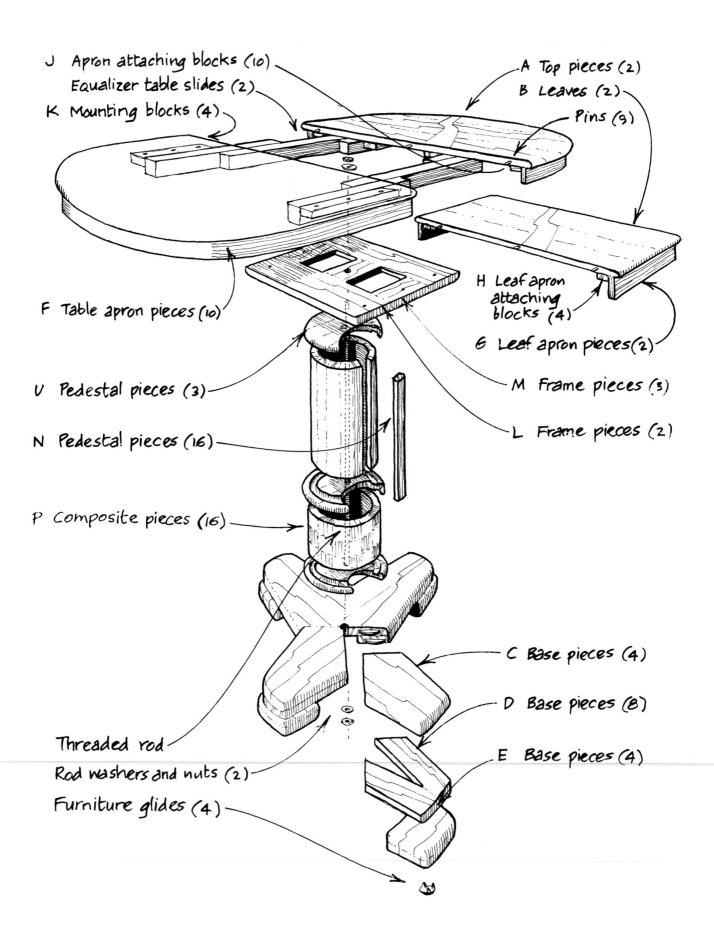

J Apron attaching blocks (10)
   Equalizer table slides (2)
K Mounting blocks (4)

A Top pieces (2)
B Leaves (2)
   Pins (9)

F Table apron pieces (10)

H Leaf apron attaching blocks (4)

G Leaf apron pieces (2)

U Pedestal pieces (3)

N Pedestal pieces (16)

M Frame pieces (3)

L Frame pieces (2)

P Composite pieces (16)

Threaded rod
Rod washers and nuts (2)
Furniture glides (4)

C Base pieces (4)

D Base pieces (8)

E Base pieces (4)

CUTTING LIST (INCHES) • maple & elm pedestal table

REF.	QTY.	PART	STOCK	THICKNESS	WIDTH	LENGTH	COMMENTS
A	2	Top pieces	Maple	3/4	26	39	Glued up from narrower stock
B	2	Leaves	Maple	3/4	12	39	
C	4	Base pieces	Maple	3/4	8	14	
D	8	Base pieces	Maple	3/4	2 1/2	11	
E	4	Base pieces	Elm	1 3/4	3 1/2	6 1/2	Glued up from narrower stock
F	10	Table apron pieces	Maple	1/8	2 3/4	75	Laminate two leaves from the 10 pieces
G	4	Leaf apron pieces	Maple	5/8	2 3/8	12	
H	4	Apron attaching blocks	Maple	3/4	1 1/8	11 7/8	
J	10	Apron attaching blocks	Maple	3/4	1 1/2	1 3/4	Includes 3/8"-long tenon at end
K	4	Mounting blocks	Maple	3/4	1	12 7/8	For mounting table slides
L	2	Frame pieces	Maple	3/4	5	22	Frame is for attaching base to slides
M	3	Frame pieces	Maple	3/4	4	22	Frame is for attaching base to slides

Pedestal

REF.	QTY.	PART	STOCK	THICKNESS	WIDTH	LENGTH	COMMENTS
N	16	Upper pieces	Maple	3/4	1 7/8	14 1/4	
P	16	Lower composite pieces	Maple/Elm	3/4	2 1/8	6 1/2	See illustration for assembly patterns
	8	Pedestal pieces	Maple	3/4	2 1/8	2	
	8	Pedestal pieces	Elm	3/4	2 1/8	2	
	6	Pedestal pieces	Maple	3/4	2 1/8	5 5/8	Extra length allows parts to be cut apart for reassembly
	6	Pedestal pieces	Elm	3/4	2 1/8	5 5/8	Extra length allows parts to be cut apart for reassembly
	4	Pedestal pieces	Maple	3/4	2 1/8	2 1/4	
	4	Pedestal pieces	Elm	3/4	2 1/8	2 1/4	
U	3	Pedestal pieces	Elm	3/4	11 1/2	11 1/2	Glued up from narrower stock and shaped round

(Rows without a REF. letter, bracketed at left: PARTS FOR LOWER COMPOSITE PIECES)

Hardware & Supplies

QTY.	ITEM
4	Metal three-prong furniture glides
9	3/8"-diameter table pins
1 pr.	26" equalizer table slides (opens for the two 12" leaves)
48	No. 20 biscuits
6	No. 6 x 1 1/2" wood screws
10	No. 6 x 1 1/4" wood screws
12	No. 8 x 1 1/4" washer head screws
12	1/2" flat washers
	3/8" threaded rod, with washers and nuts

LOWER PEDESTAL ASSEMBLY PATTERNS • INCHES

2 1/4" Maple	2" Elm	5 5/8" Maple	2" Elm	5 5/8" Maple	2" Elm	5 5/8" Maple	2" Elm	2 1/4" Maple

Make two of each of these assemblies.

2 1/4" Elm	2" Maple	5 5/8" Elm	2" Maple	5 5/8" Elm	2" Maple	5 5/8" Elm	2" Maple	2 1/4" Elm

CUTTING LIST (MILLIMETERS) • **maple & elm pedestal table**

REF.	QTY.	PART	STOCK	THICKNESS	WIDTH	LENGTH	COMMENTS
A	2	Top pieces	Maple	19	660	990	Glued up from narrower stock
B	2	Leaves	Maple	19	305	990	
C	4	Base pieces	Maple	19	200	355	
D	8	Base pieces	Maple	19	65	280	
E	4	Base pieces	Elm	45	90	165	Glued up from narrower stock
F	10	Table apron pieces	Maple	3	70	1905	Laminate two leaves from the 10 pieces
G	4	Leaf apron pieces	Maple	16	60	305	
H	4	Apron attaching blocks	Maple	19	29	301	
J	10	Apron attaching blocks	Maple	19	38	45	Includes 10mm-long tenon at end
K	4	Mounting blocks	Maple	19	25	325	For mounting table slides
L	2	Frame pieces	Maple	19	125	560	Frame is for attaching base to slides
M	3	Frame pieces	Maple	19	100	560	Frame is for attaching base to slides

Pedestal

REF.	QTY.	PART	STOCK	THICKNESS	WIDTH	LENGTH	COMMENTS
N	16	Upper pieces	Maple	19	47	360	
P	16	Lower composite pieces	Maple/Elm	19	54	164	See illustration for assembly patterns
PARTS FOR LOWER COMPOSITE PIECES	8	Pedestal pieces	Maple	19	54	50	
	8	Pedestal pieces	Elm	19	54	50	
	6	Pedestal pieces	Maple	19	54	145	Extra length allows parts to be cut apart for reassembly
	6	Pedestal pieces	Elm	19	54	145	Extra length allows parts to be cut apart for reassembly
	4	Pedestal pieces	Maple	19	54	57	
	4	Pedestal pieces	Elm	19	54	57	
U	3	Pedestal pieces	Elm	19	290	290	Glued up from narrower stock and shaped round

Hardware & Supplies

4	Metal three-prong furniture glides
9	10mm-diameter table pins
1 pr.	660mm equalizer table slides (opens for the two 305mm leaves)
48	No. 20 biscuits
6	No. 6 x 38mm wood screws
10	No. 6 x 32mm wood screws
12	No. 8 x 32mm washer head screws
12	13mm flat washers
	10mm threaded rod, with washers and nuts

LOWER PEDESTAL ASSEMBLY PATTERNS • MILLIMETERS

57 Maple	50 Elm	145 Maple	50 Elm	145 Maple	50 Elm	145 Maple	50 Elm	57 Maple

Make two of each of these assemblies.

57 Elm	50 Maple	145 Elm	50 Maple	145 Elm	50 Maple	145 Elm	50 Maple	57 Elm

1 Cut and sand a piece of scrap plywood to make a template for shaping the top. The single piece laid out four ways forms a near oval shape. It need not be an exact oval. Mine is shaped to allow more comfortable seating at the ends of the table. First cut it on the band saw and then, using a sanding disc in the table saw, sand it smooth.

2 Use a pencil to trace the shape of the template on the tabletop parts, then cut the shape with the band saw. I cut just outside the line to allow for accurate cleanup with the router.

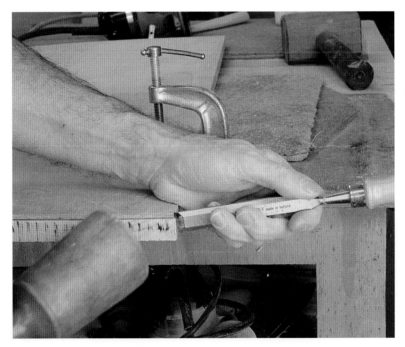

4 With a 1/2" mortise clean-up bit in the router, follow the template to begin cutting the edge to shape.

3 Clamp the template to the tabletop and use a straight chisel to cut in line with the template to prevent router tear-out. An alternate method would be to clamp a piece of scrap wood in place as shown when making Jean's cherry dining table (see step 10 on page 89).

5 With the template removed, the mortise clean-up bit follows the previous cut to finish the edge. Lower the cutter in steps.

6 Clamp the two tabletop halves together for belt sanding the edges.

7 Use a doweling jig to drill holes for the table alignment pins.

8 With the alignment pins in place and the tabletop parts held together, rout the edges.

9 Use a random-orbit sander to sand the edges.

10 To begin forming the cylinder, glue elm and maple blocks together. It takes careful planning to make the squares come out the right size. I used the sled on the table saw to cut them to accurate length and planned for an extra ¼" at each end to fit dadoes in the cylinder caps.

11 Use a bar clamp to hold the elm and maple parts together as the glue sets.

12 Use the table saw to cut the sections to the correct angle. I made a practice cut on a strip of scrap wood, then cut the strip into sections to check the accuracy of my angle before cutting the maple and elm block.

maple & elm **pedestal table**

13 Cut the assembled strips into shorter sections that will form the cylinder.

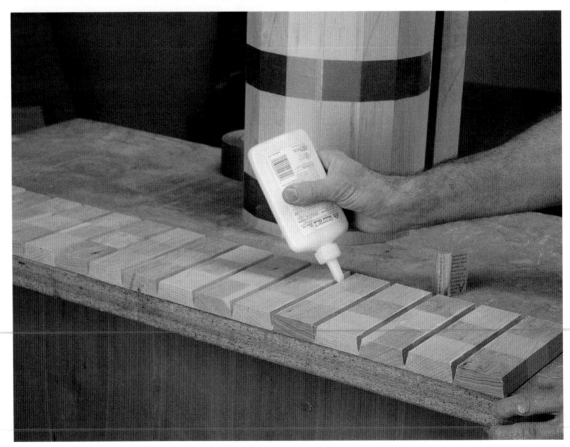

14 Use duct tape to hold the strips together for gluing. I align the pieces outside up, apply the tape and turn the assembled unit over for spreading the glue. A folded business card works well for spreading the glue into the joints.

108

15 Roll the glued assembly up, then use a band clamp to pull the pieces tight, as shown in these two photos.

16 As an alternate method, stretchy package-sealing tape can be used in place of band clamps. Each wrap applies more pressure to the assembled column.

MAKING A CYLINDER LATHE

My cylinder lathe, unlike conventional lathes, is made to turn at low speeds by hand, with the router removing stock in place of conventional lathe tools. In addition to making cylinders from hardwood for tables, this cylinder lathe, because it turns slowly, can safely make quarter and half cylinders as well. It uses conventional V-belt pulleys to guide the router along a hardwood track. I use screws to attach end plates to glued up cylinders, which spin on axles made from ½" bolts.

Make the cut in a series of passes, moving the router bit deeper into the cut each time. I make a full revolution of the cylinder then move the router slightly for the next revolution. It is not a speedy process, but one that gives an accurately milled cylinder for those not having a conventional lathe large enough to handle the mass.

To make quarter or half columns is easy. Just forget to glue the sections where the quarters or halves meet. The screws attaching the sections to the end places will hold them for accurate turning.

A belt sander held in place is used to remove marks from milling. By holding the belt sander at a slight angle, the cylinder spins for even sanding.

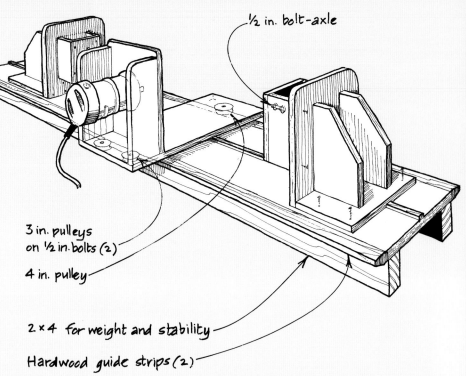

½ in. bolt-axle

3 in. pulleys on ½ in. bolts (2)

4 in. pulley

2 x 4 for weight and stability

Hardwood guide strips (2)

17 With waferboard end pieces screwed in place, fit the assembled columns into the cylinder lathe. I use both hands to keep control of the cylinder as the router cuts. I turn the cylinder one revolution, then move the router for another cut. I rout to the finished size in several steps.

18 After the column is routed round, use a belt sander to remove the milling marks left by the router. Holding the belt sander at a slight angle makes the cylinder turn for even sanding.

19 The random-orbit sander also turns the cylinder while doing the finish sanding.

20 To make the end caps for the cylinders, start with square stock. I glued mine with alternating grain orientation. Drill a pilot hole in the center and use it to guide the drilling of a guide pin for the band saw. Clamp plywood to the band saw top after cutting a slot for the blade.

22 Use the sanding disc in the table saw to sand the edges smooth. Hold the stock very firmly and take a small cut in order to maintain control. Turn the stock counter-clockwise into the sanding disc.

21 Place the square stock over the guide pin and cut the round end caps. After cutting the end caps on the band saw, the same jig is useful on the table saw and router table in the following steps. The drill bit used to make the holes becomes useful as the guide pin.

23 With the same guide pin arrangement inverted and clamped to the router table, lower the end caps over the guide pin and router bit to cut the channels for the cylinders to fit.

24 To begin making the aprons for the table, lay out the shape of the top on particleboard using the same template used in making the tabletop. Then carefully measure for the placement of the blocks.

25 Screw blocks to the particleboard for clamping the laminating strips in place.

26 Carefully spread glue on both sides of the strips.

27 Wrap the sandwich of strips onto the gluing jig. I use spring clamps to hold the ends in place while C-clamps are tightened. Starting at the center, work your way to the ends.

28 Using nearly all the clamps in my shop, I place clamps between the guide blocks as well.

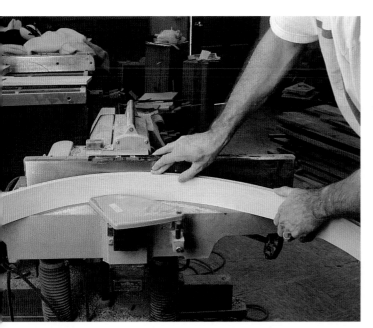

29 After the glue has dried and the clamps are removed, use the jointer to clean up one edge. This is a tricky operation requiring a great deal of care and attention. A carefully positioned outfeed roller can help.

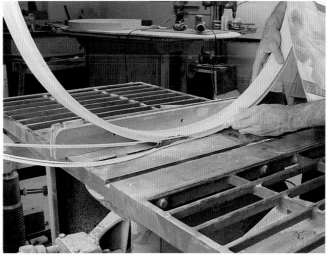

30 With the jointed edge against the fence, cut the opposite side of the aprons on the table saw. This requires a steady hand and slow feed.

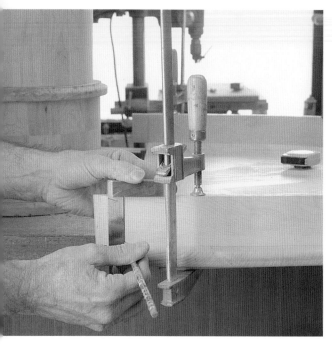

31 With the aprons clamped in position to the tabletop, mark for cutting them to length.

32 Use the sled on the table saw to cut the aprons to fit.

33 Use a roundover bit in the handheld router to rout the aprons.

34 To begin making the base unit, miter the base parts using the miter sled.

35 Cut the additional parts using the miter guide on the table saw, then use the table saw sled to cut where they fit together.

36 Use a brad nailer to pin the parts together to keep them from sliding as the clamps are tightened.

38 I often use found objects to mark shapes on wood. Here, a 12" sanding disc is useful in marking the shape of the base.

37 Trim the base parts to match using the band saw. Leave a small amount to be sanded away.

39 Use the sanding disc in the table saw to sand the edges to match.

40 Rout and sand the edges prior to assembly.

41 Use a biscuit joiner to prepare the base for assembly.

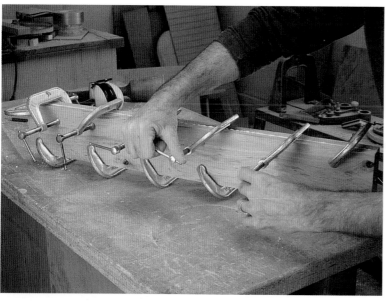

42 Glue ⁷⁄₈"-thick elm boards together to begin forming the feet.

43 Cut and shape the feet using the band saw, then use a drum sander to finish the inside shape.

44 Check the feet for fit and proportion.

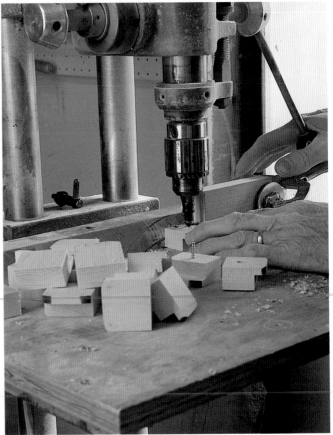

45 Make blocks for attaching the aprons to the tabletop. Carefully plan the depth of countersink to match the length of screws being used to keep from passing through the tabletop.

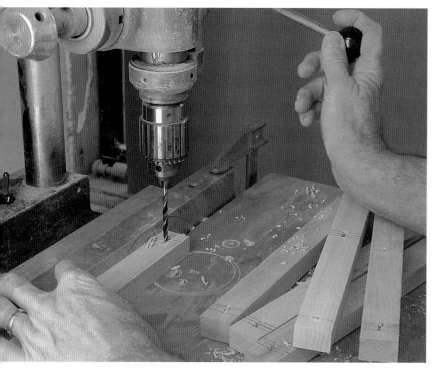

47 Assemble the upper framework for attaching the base to the table slides using biscuits.

46 Drill holes in the attachment blocks. Note that holes are elongated to allow for expansion and contraction. These blocks will be attached to the table slides as in making Jean's Cherry Dining Table.

48 Use Danish oil to finish most of the parts prior to assembly.

49 After oiling with Danish oil, use spray satin polyurethane on both sides of the tabletop. The spray satin finish, carefully applied, gives a more durable surface for regular use.

51 With nuts and washers at the bottom, stack the layers in place. After assembly, use a hacksaw to cut the rod to the right length.

50 To begin assembling the column, drill a hole in each piece for the ³⁄₈" threaded rod to pass through.

52 Use blocks to attach the aprons to the top. The end blocks are glued to the aprons. The others are left loose to allow for the top to expand and contract.

53 With the aprons in place, accurately locate the position for the pedestal to fit the table slides. Then screw the pedestal assembly to the slides and the slides to the tabletop.

a gallery of work

It is a marvel to me that people are willing to commission work, having enough confidence in woodworkers to allow them to make things they've never made before, with so little certainty as to the results. It is not surprising that most of my furniture commissions have grown from very special relationships with remarkable people.

The idea that one should not mix business with pleasure is wrong. My work always has been infused with the pleasure of friendship, and each piece describes not only form and technique but relationship with family and friends.

This walnut end table was made for my Aunt Wuzzie and Uncle Newt very early in my woodworking career. The commission was inspired by their interest in encouraging me in my work and was more an act of love than of need in a home already full of antiques. It is made to reflect the classic Japanese torii architectural form, the gateway to a shinto temple. As in Japanese architecture, the table is made with exposed mortise-and-tenon joints, wedged with cherry to lock the joints in position.

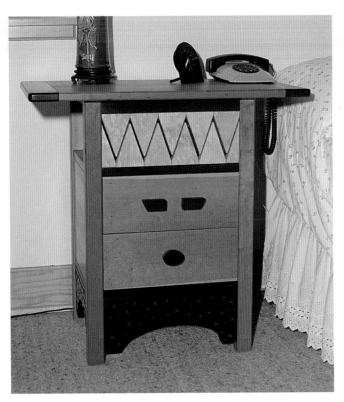

This cherry bedside table was commissioned by a close friend, artist and businessman and was inspired by the kachinas of the pueblo tribes in the American Southwest. I don't know how many people would want such an animated spirit at their bedsides, but designing it was a process of play. Each of us took turns with pen and paper to arrive at the final design.

In a related cherry and maple hall table, carved spirals, triangles and routed holes reflect the symbolism of native cultures. The black areas are ebonized using a chemical solution of steel wool dissolved in vinegar.

My cherry dining table, chairs and sideboard were featured in *Woodworker's Journal* in 1997 and were done for a cousin and her husband. The tabletop expands with leaves at each end. The open area at the center allows for expansion and contraction of the solid cherry wood used in the tabletop.

This bird's-eye maple and cherry dining table was the predecessor to the maple and elm table shown in this book.

This table and bench set is titled "We Traveled Rivers." It commemorates the time when rivers were the primary form of transportation in Arkansas. I created it as part of a traveling exhibit titled "The Lost Roads Project," which consisted of works by Arkansas writers and poets. The project toured the state for two years. This set was commissioned to provide a reading place within the exhibit area where visitors could sit and read the text of the exhibit in the usual way ... from a book. The top of the table features a "river channel" filled with loose stones, which I gathered from various Arkansas rivers during canoe trips. This work was featured in the April 1996 issue of *Fine Woodworking*. The table and benches are made from "quilted" sugar maple and were designed for easy disassembly, crating and transporting between exhibits. Because "level" is an imaginary concept in my Ozark Mountains portion of the state, one leg of the table is cut shorter than the rest and is perched on a little rock, a pun on the Arkansas state capital, Little Rock.

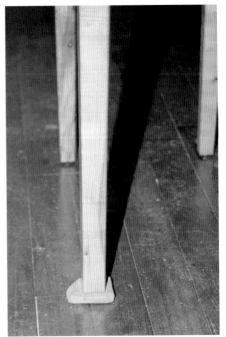

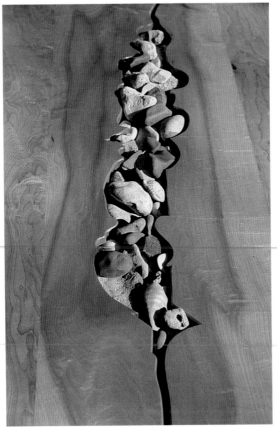

index

More great furniture projects from
Popular Woodworking Books!

Northwoods furniture is functional and solidly built, embodying everything you value about life away from the fast-paced world. These 13 step-by-step projects can give you that kind of life with just a weekend in the woodshop. Each project uses basic woodshop tools, time-tested construction techniques and a variety of attractive woods.

ISBN 1-55870-569-4, paperback, 128 pages, #70500-K

Turn your woodshop scrap lumber into simple, inexpensive pieces of furniture that are both sturdy and attractive. These 15 intriguing projects include a wide variety of tables, a bedspread valet, a desk, a mirror frame and more. Author and woodworker Armand Sussman's project assembly methods are unique, using only a few saw cuts and glue.

ISBN 1-55870-543-0, paperback, 128 pages, #70404-K

Transform any room into the perfect workspace! Inside you'll find invaluable tips and advice, plus 15 fresh, functional, fun-to-build projects packed with detailed photographs and step-by-step instructions. Designs range from simple storage modules to a computer desk/workstation, so no matter what your level of skill, you'll find plenty of woodshop excitement.

ISBN 1-55870-561-9, paperback, 128 pages, #70489-K

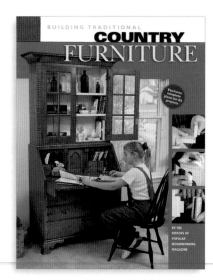

Add charm to your home and new life to your woodshop with these exciting, attractive projects! Each one is faithful to the country furniture tradition, mixing classic lines with straightforward construction techniques. You'll find an incredible range of designs, some simple but clever, others exquisite and heirloom-worthy.

ISBN 1-55870-585-6, paperback, 128 pages, #70521-K

These books and other fine Popular Woodworking titles are available from your local bookstore, online supplier or by calling 1-800-221-5831.